Kay - I'm honored to call you my "sister!" Jeanette Levellie

The Heart of Humor:

Sixty Helpings of Hilarity to Nourish Your Soul

Jeanette Levellie

Drawings by Ron Levellie

$10—

Elk Lake Publishing

The Heart of Humor: Sixty Helpings of Hilarity to Nourish Your Soul

Requests for information should be addressed to:
Elk Lake Publishing, Atlanta, GA 30024
ISBN-13: 978-1942513018
ISBN-10: 1942513011

Cover and graphics design: Fred St. Laurent
Editing: Deb Haggerty and Kathi Macias
EBook conversions: Fred St. Laurent
Drawings by Ron Levellie
Published in association with Diana Flegal, agent, Hartline Literary Agency

ENDORSEMENTS

"Jeanette Levellie has the spiritual gift of encouragement. She shares it in her conversations, her ministry outreach, and now in this entertaining and enlightening book *The Heart of Humor.* As you read, you'll smile and chuckle, but at the same time you'll gain insights on life, love, and relationships."

Dr. Dennis E. Hensley, author, *The Power of Positive Productivity

"You'll laugh. You'll learn. You'll be entertained. And, you'll be encouraged."

***James Watkins, author, speaker, threat to society**

"Whether she's writing about her "Maggie Moments," planting onions on top of onions, or her favorite sport—dining out—Jeanette Levellie's *The Heart of Humor* delights and inspires. Do yourself a favor and read it."

Bob Hostetler, author of *The Red Letter Life

"Jeanette Levellie is funny from her carrot top to the bottom of her perfectly-coordinated fashion shoes. And she has a way of looking at life with a slant that helps us share in her humor. Even if you don't own a cat, you'll laugh your way through *The Heart of Humor.* I sure did!"

Debbie Hardy, Queen of Resilience and author of *Stepping through Cancer* and *Free to Be Fabulous.

"I joke that Jeanette's last name should be Lovely instead of Levellie. With a heart filled with love & overflowing with humor, and a desire for people to see Jesus, Jeanette is active in the lives of her readers. You'll love her as a friend as she communicates God's truth and love in practical ways."

***Elaine W. Miller, Author/Speaker, http://www.SplashesofSerenity.com**

"Jeanette combines wisdom and gentle humor to mend tattered souls. Her sweet spirit and selfless attitude rest upon her readers like a nurse's reassuring hand. She is one of the most compassionate, encouraging Christians you will ever meet."

Cammie Quinn, author of *That I May See Him

"Jeanette Levellie proves once again that "laughing at ourselves is a way of loving ourselves," and fulfills her promise to nourish our souls. Helpings of humor include "I Love My Hips," "How to Host the Perfect Pity Party," and my personal favorite, "Quit Pinching My Fruit." The last bite of each *Helping of Hilarity* is labeled "From My Heart to Yours," uplifting comments that add a taste of dessert following Jeanette's witty vignettes. Once you partake of these *Helpings of Hilarity*, you will be nourished as I was by the humorous, Spirit-filled heart of the author."

***Clella Camp, Christian author/speaker, *Just Walking* by AMG publishers**

DEDICATION

To my daughter, ***Marie***:
A star in the night, a song of joy, a humble encourager
&
To my son, ***Ron***:
A valiant man, a lover of wisdom, a faithful friend
Thanks for being
Exactly
You

ACKNOWLEDGMENTS

One of my heroes, the late Fred Rogers, wrote a song entitled "I'm Proud of You." I'd like to thank the following additional heroes who've said to me in various ways, "I'm proud of you."

My hero in love, Kevin, who reminds me of Jesus more than anyone I know. You get the biggest trophy!

Heroes in prayer Marie Adams, Beth Gormong, Dee Stark, Cecelia Lester, Susan Reinhardt, Karen Lange, Doris Kidgell (my mom).

My ever-encouraging, fun-loving, brilliant hero-agent, Diana Flegal.

Publishing heroes Fred St. Laurent, Kathi Macias, and Deb Haggerty at Elk Lake—I have nothing but praise for your professionalism and grace.

My heroes in faith Diana Savage, Cecil Murphey, Cammie Quinn, Beverly Mathieson, Kathy Nobilione, Kenneth Hagin, Sr., and Carol Drey.

Editing heroes Diana Savage, James Watkins, and Ken Ramstead. I love how you make me sound smarter than I am!

Cheerleading heroes Clella Camp, Betty Kelly, Lin Johnson, Gina Paris, Barb Snyder, Gayle Rayhel, and Veronica Apple.

My heroes of humor Ron Levellie, James Watkins, the late Erma Bombeck, Rhonda Schrock, Torry Martin, and my laughter-inducing grandkids, Jenessa, Daniel, and Alyssa Adams.

Mostly I thank my #1 hero, Jesus, for looking into this redhead and seeing beyond the nuttiness. Someday—very soon, I hope—I will place my crown of jewels at Your feet, look into Your eyes, and laugh my loudest, the best way I can think of to say, "I'm proud of YOU."

With love and thanks,

Jen

Foreword

What? You're actually reading the foreword? Nobody reads forewords—unless you're a major exception. You're obviously an intelligent, discriminating reader who reads the acknowledgements and endnotes as well. So I suppose I should make this worth your while and fulfill my honors, privileges, and prescribed duties as a foreword writer.

First, a foreword needs to be written by someone who is revered in the book's field and well-respected by the genre's readership. So by placing his name on the cover, this will cause the potential reader browsing the thousands of offerings at the local bookstore/coffee shop to put down the copy of *Martha Stewart's Home Dentistry* book and pick up *The Heart of Humor* instead. "Oh, I see Mr. Smarty Pants Author wrote the foreword, so I must immediately purchase this book!"

So once again, a major exception! Well, I have written a text book on writing humor, *Writing with Banana Peels*, and have taught the subject at colleges and conferences. Plus I wrote a humor column for fifteen years in three newspapers. And I've won some book awards, so there is a slight possibly that a handful of people might be persuaded to buy this book simply based on "Foreword by James Watkins: Author, Speaker, Threat to Society." I hope my mom will buy it.

Second, a foreword needs to point out all the wonderful things about the author that she, being the humble soul that she is, could not possibly bring herself to write. This, however, is no exception.

I discovered Jeanette at a writers' conferences several years ago. Well, you don't really "discover" Jeanette. You experience Jeanette! The energetic redhead with a flair for fashion bursts on the scene with a wake of joyful laughter trailing behind her. You simply cannot ignore her.

She quickly became one of my favorite authors for the magazine I edit. I actually laughed out loud reading the first manuscript she showed me, which could be grounds for losing my membership card in "The Society of Grumpy, Dream-Crushing Editors." I rarely, if ever LOL! Truly funny writers are extremely rare in Christian publishing, but Jeanette is a wonderful exception. She is wise and witty, whacky and warm in her writing. She can put the "fun" back in a fundamentalist!

And third, a foreword needs to close the sale. So put down whatever other books you have in your arms or those in your online "shopping cart" and buy *this* book (unless, of course, one of those other books is one of mine; then buy them *both*!). You'll laugh. You'll learn. You'll be entertained. And you'll be encouraged.

Now, on to the real reason you bought this book: sixty helping of hilarity to nourish your soul.

James Watkins: Author, Speaker, Threat to Society

Chapter 1
I Love My Hips

For the first time in decades, as the holidays approach, I'm not worried about my hips getting larger. I love my hips. I feel sorry for all those skinny-as-a-preacher's-wallet supermodels slinking down the runway in their pencil skirts. They've never discovered the splendid uses of hips.

In my hipless days, if I wanted to tote a box of Christmas decorations from the backyard shed to the house, I had to carry it in both arms, like a hug. The situation made navigating across the yard a bit rough since I couldn't see where I was stepping. Now I simply perch the box on one hip, breeze across the yard, open the door with my free hand, and collapse into the room.

Hips are also useful for bouncing hungry or colicky babies while stirring a pot of macaroni on the stove. Without hips you'd have to plunk Junior or Princess in a highchair and listen to the wails while you tried to fix supper. A ton of macaroni has been rescued from burning by the marvelous invention of hips.

On a recent visit to see my grandchildren, I discovered my favorite use for hips. I sat on a playground swing and realized there was no danger of falling out, no matter how high I flew. My handy hips had me wedged in tighter than a stepsister's foot in a Cinderella slipper. But I knew I'd never revert to being hipless again when my six-year-old grandson stepped behind me to push. In his innocent voice he said, "Grandma, you're easy to push because your bum is so big!"

That's why you won't find me refusing mashed potatoes or eggnog this holiday season. How can I let my little guy down? I do wish I could find a way to get out of this swing, though.

♥ *From My Heart to Yours: Although I believe God wants me to care for my body as His temple, I refuse to fall for society's lie that my worth stems from how I look. Gratitude for my hips and exercising daily make a healthy, happy combination.*

Chapter 2
Whiskery Wisdom

Cats: most people either hate or love them. The haters contend that felines ruin furniture, kill songbirds, and consider people their slaves. The lovers argue that cats control rodents, relieve stress, and cover up their poops.

I find my "spoiled brats in fur suits" brimming with wisdom. Here are some insights I've learned from the roguish angels:

❖ If you fight with the other household cats, you won't have energy left to ward off enemy cats.

❖ It's okay to have whiskers and pointy ears.

❖ Look for a patch of sunshine, and stay there.

❖ Naps are cool.

❖ Don't fuss about your food, or the one who feeds you may start buying a cheaper brand.

❖ Purring will get you everywhere.

❖ Master the "Shocked and Innocent Look" if someone laughs at you. Better yet stick your nose in the air and saunter away, pretending you don't care.

❖ Naps are fun.

❖ Act as if you know what you're doing even if you don't have a clue.

❖ Convince those around you how blessed they are to live in the same universe with you.

❖ Refuse to give up; if one bird escapes, climb another tree.

❖ Naps are refreshing.

Similar to cats people are a mix of aggravating and endearing qualities. When I'm tempted to dismiss a brother or sister as too ornery to tolerate, I remember how God bears with my faults and stupid mistakes. Receiving His unconditional love frees me to love myself and others, focusing on positive qualities. Now if I could only convince my husband to see the good in our kitties….

♥ *From My Heart to Yours: I believe God gave us pets to help us laugh more. Whether you like dogs in tutus, cats hanging by their claws from tree branches, or pygmy marmosets yodeling to their friends, observing animals is one of the most relaxing, fun activities on earth.*

Chapter 3
How Do I Annoy Thee?

How can a person make noise getting underwear out of a drawer? My husband's invented a way.

In my extra-large kitchen, how can he always need to be in the same spot and at the same moment as I? He's figured that out, too.

Can he listen to high-pitched snippets of irritating music as he downloads music to his MP3 player when I'm gone to work all day and he has the house to himself? Oh, no. He must do this never-ending job when I'm home, trying to concentrate on writing a deeply spiritual article in the next room.

When I've teased him about lying awake nights inventing new

ways to annoy me, he disagrees. "I don't have to invent new ways; I irritate you without trying."

I recently discovered how he devises all these bothersome habits of his that seem to multiply daily as he ages. He is the founder and lifetime president of the Annoyance-of-the-Hour Club for Men.

He never upset me when we were dating and engaged. Well, maybe once a week or so, but it was easy to overlook the wee little quirks that everyone must have. Love and passion trumped those prickly little frustrations hardly worth mentioning. Until the honeymoon. While I was sleeping, washing my hair, or glancing at the moon, he called the first meeting of the AHCM, with only himself in attendance. And he's been thinking up new ways to bug me ever since.

When I'm gone to Bible study on Friday nights, he holds meetings of the other men who belong to his club—all married men—and they share their secrets and new discoveries.

"I found out that when I trim my toenails during her favorite TV show, it drives her nutso."

"Dude, that's nothing. You need to trim them when her mother is visiting. Or better yet, don't trim them at all, and then stab her with them just as she's dropping off to sleep."

I can imagine the backslaps and high fives when one of them comes up with an original annoyance.

"Hey, you guys know how we decided to start mumbling to ourselves all over the house? I discovered this week that humming the same tune hundreds of times in one day works much better. They can ignore the mumbling after a while, but the humming drives them crazy. Especially if there's no definable rhythm or melody. Just make something up with the same six notes over and over." They then practice for each other, perfecting their hums until they reach the pinnacle of irksomeness.

Next on the agenda comes smacking, slurping, and spilling of the noisiest snacks and drinks they could find, and then closing their eyes to the leftover mess.

They end the meeting with a secret oath to work harder at grating on their wives' nerves, to proselytize every new husband they meet, and to teach their sons from infancy how to develop exasperating habits.

I thought of starting my own club for women so we could retaliate. But after two minutes of consideration, I realized none of us would live long enough to catch up, let alone beat them at their own game. I'm forced to concede that as creative as we are, we women cannot hold a drippy candle to the ways men find to annoy.

♥ *From My Heart to Yours: I sometimes wonder, does my husband annoy me, or do I give up my peace by allowing his habits to irritate me? Will we have quirks in heaven? If so, we'll either ignore them or laugh at them.*

Chapter 4
Everybody Loves Dummies

One thing that always makes me laugh is to read about dumb criminals. My husband recently bought me a book by Leland Gregory entitled *The Stupid Crook Book* (Andrews McMeel, 2002). Here are a few of my favorite stories:

❖ A Texas man broke into a residence, making a clean getaway with a TV. He was caught a few hours later reentering the premises; he'd come back to steal the remote control he forgot the first time around.

❖ When a man robbed a liquor store in New Mexico, he thought he'd stumped the police by wearing a bag over his head. But he failed on one little point, giving the police a clear description of him—the bag was clear plastic.

❖ A man who got a ticket for driving without a license submitted to a routine search. When authorities found cocaine in his underwear, he tried to give them a snow job by claiming that the underwear didn't belong to him.

❖ A woman tried to cash a check in a Durham, North Carolina, bank. But the check wasn't made out to her or any other person. It read, "Tension Envelope Company." The woman claimed her name was Mrs. Tension Envelope. The teller put the check in an envelope and called the police. Now she had some serious tension on her hands….

❖ A man in Detroit Lakes, Minnesota, was charged with the attempted robbery of a convenience store. According to prosecutors the thief stopped a customer on his way into the store and handed him a dollar. The robber told the man he wanted to rob the store but didn't have a good disguise. He then asked the fellow to do him a favor and buy him a handkerchief to cover his face. The customer took the dollar, walked into the store, and told the clerk about the odd encounter outside; the clerk called the police. We still don't know who ended up with the dollar.

❖ When a young entrepreneur in Baltimore, Maryland, put up a sign on the side of a newspaper box announcing his wares, two plainclothes police officers approached him. They asked if he had posted the sign. "Sure," he said. "It's the best way I've figured out to get people to stop." His sales-boosting sign offered $10-bags of marijuana.

❖ A man in Hamburg, Germany, was suffering from amnesia. He stopped into the police station and asked for help in finding his identity. He realized his mistake when the police discovered that he was wanted for fraud and arrested him.

❖ And one of my favorite bumper stickers reads, "My son was Inmate of the Month at San Mateo County Jail."

♥ *From My Heart to Yours: I think it's poetic justice when a criminal gets caught due to his or her stupidity. But I also feel compassion for them, since I'd be in their shoes if not for the grace of God and the blood of Jesus.*

Chapter 5
The Not-So-Easy-Bake Oven Escapade

Aunt Lois and Uncle Jack bought me the toy of my dreams, an Easy-Bake Oven, the year I was eight. I had wanted one for forever (well, a year or so) and couldn't wait to try it out. Two days later I was down the block at my friend Kathy's, where we strung an extension cord out to the driveway to make our dainty delicacies. Kathy's mom had voted us out of her kitchen for who knows what crazy reason.

After only twenty minutes of baking delight, my older brother, Danny, came over, shouting that Mom wanted me on the phone. I hurried up the street, wondering why Mom was calling from work in the middle of the day on our Christmas vacation. Maybe she just wanted to have me get something out of the freezer for supper.

Instead I got an earful. "Danny says you are strewing your Easy-Bake Oven stuff all over Kathy's parents' driveway. Clean that up and get it home this instant. I'm sure Aunt Lois and Uncle Jack did not intend you to be traipsing all over the neighborhood making messes with that toy. They spent a lot of money on that…."

I tried to argue, explaining we'd made only one or two recipes, and Danny was totally exaggerating about the mess. But Mom refused to listen. I dejectedly walked back to Kathy's, picked up my oven, and toted it home. Conveniently Danny blipped out of the universe for the next two hours until Mom would be home to prevent me from poisoning his Kool-Aid with dish soap or putting thumbtacks on the toilet seat.

Because he was the only male in the family for several years between Mom's two marriages, he felt it his duty to enforce his reign of terror over me. The Easy-Bake Oven Escapade was only one in a long line of tactics meant to intimidate the short redheaded sister. I shudder at the memory of Arm-Behind-Back Torture in the backseat while Mom was in the grocery store; Waiting-at-Bathroom-Door-in-the-Dark-with-Terrifying-Stone-faced-Look; and Blood-Congealing-Maniacal-Laugh-at-Odd-Moments to scare the pants off of me.

We youngest may have been spoiled with extra toys, later bedtimes, and more of Mom and Dad's money when we went to college, but we paid for it in our earlier years by the torture imposed on us from above. I haven't done the research, but I'll bet you my Easy-Bake Oven that Genghis Kahn was an older brother.

Danny passed away last January. He's probably training the older angels how to give the younger ones noogies and the best times to tattle to God. I wish I could be there to hear it. I also wish I could have Danny back here for an hour or two. I'd hold his arm behind his back and make him cry uncle for me just once.

♥ *From My Heart to Yours: As children, we view siblings as a curse. With the perspective of an adult, we realize what blessings they are. If you have a sibling, don't wait until it's too late to say, "I appreciate you."*

Chapter 6
Woolly Worm Report

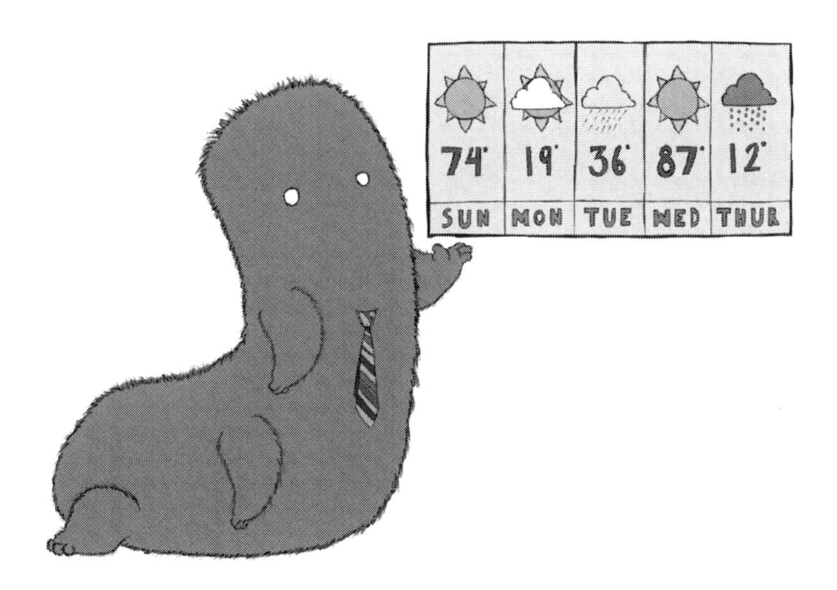

When we moved from Los Angeles to Paris, Illinois, thirteen years ago, someone asked me what I thought of the winters here. Wrapping the third scarf around my neck and adjusting my earmuffs, I said, "I try not to think about them too much."

Not that spinning off the icy highway into a ditch isn't my idea of a fun new game. Or that I don't enjoy drinking seventeen cups of tea a day from November to March; I always did like that burst of energy a strong cup of tea provides. I even discovered a brand of long underwear made from silk so I didn't have to buy clothes two sizes larger than usual. That's always gratifying.

Did you know there is a surefire way to predict winter weather? According to early American folklore, you can forecast the harshness of an upcoming winter by examining the brown band around a woolly worm's middle. The thinner the brownish-red band, the harsher winter will be.

But I have my own methods. As we go on a walk up the country lane near our home and I spot a woolly worm scooting across the pavement, I'll note its coloration. If the worm is dark brown or black, representing the bare earth, I predict a mild winter with no snow. If it's orange—a happy, warm color—I maintain the upcoming winter will be warmer than usual. And if the woolly worm is white or tan, I report that winter will be fast and fun, with snowfall only on Christmas Eve.

Scientific? Hardly. Accurate? Rarely. But my overly-biased woolly worm reports make us laugh every time. And giggles help us get through the long, freezing months better than gripes. I imagine even the woolly worms laugh. At me.

> ♥ *From My Heart to Yours: I may not be able to predict the weather, but I'm convinced the Apostle John predicted accurately when he told us Jesus is coming soon. I hope you and I will spend eternity together with Him, in that lovely city where every day is bright, and every woolly worm gives a sunny report.*

Chapter 7
Missing the Mister

Whenever my husband flies out of town for a few days, I think of all the distractions that will go with him. *No loud Southern Gospel music. No bumping into each other in the kitchen or his snoring waking me up twice a night. I'll sit in my office and write articles, listen to nothing but birdsong, and sleep the night through.*

We chat all the way to the airport, and our kiss at the curb lasts extra-long. On the way home I sing and grin, anticipating the next four days of A Little Piece of Quiet.

When I sort the mail that afternoon, I silently toss my husband's correspondence into his empty recliner. *It seems odd not to hear music or see the TV on. Oh, well, all the quiet will help me concentrate on my writing.*

I eat alone while reading the paper. *News isn't much fun when there's no one to complain about it with. Oh, well, he'll be home in four days. I'll save up my gripes 'til then.*

Sleep comes slowly with that vacant pillow and half a bed beside me. Although my four cats fill up the empty space, they refuse to snore. I wake up five times during the night.

Over the next three days, I finish a book I'm working on, write several articles, and never once bump into anyone in my kitchen. But I notice I'm telling the checker at the market a lot more information than she wants to hear. And I'm tired from lack of sleep.

Finally my vacation ends, and I rush to the airport, my heart aglow.

"How'd it go?" he says as we wait for his luggage.

I squeeze his arm, smile, and say, "Oh, fine. But next time I'm Coming with you."

♥ *From My Heart to Yours: In healthy relationships, short absences from each other help us appreciate more and take less for granted. God knit our hearts together, but didn't join us at the hips!*

Chapter 8
So Who Invented Laughter, Anyway?

In a smelly, damp cave eons ago, someone concocted the thought that God is against laughter and wants His kids to take everything seriously. That person is dead now, so we can toss out his or her notion of God as a disagreeable deity. Here's the proof that He is the inventor of laughter:

"Abraham was a hundred years old when his son Isaac was born to him. Sarah said, *'God has brought me laughter, and everyone who hears about this will laugh with me'*" (Genesis 21:5–6, emphasis mine).

So… God must think it funny to give a baby to a 100-year-old man and his ninety-year-old bride. Because this meant the end of Sarah's shame and the fulfillment of God's promise to the couple, she laughed right along with the Almighty.

"The One enthroned in heaven laughs; the Lord scoffs at them" (Psalm 2:4).

This is the Lord's response to heathen leaders who boast of freeing themselves from the kingship of God. The Message renders this verse, "Heaven-throned GOD breaks out laughing…amused at their presumption."

Later in the Psalms when Saul stalks David in order to kill him, David writes, "But you, GOD, break out laughing; you treat the godless nations like jokes" (Psalm 59:8, MSG). How merciful of the Lord to show David He was not afraid of the plots of the wicked and He had David's back. He proves His confidence by laughing.

"For everything its season, and for every activity under heaven its time: …a time to weep and a time to laugh; a time for mourning and a time for dancing" (Ecclesiastes 3:1, 4, NEB).

Oh, the splendid balance in the heart of God! His calendar allows for laughter as well as tears, dancing as well as mourning. Now if I could just convince my husband that square dancing is a divine inspiration….

"And now, GOD, do it again—bring rains to our drought-stricken lives So those who planted their crops in despair will shout hurrahs at the harvest, So those who went off with heavy hearts will come home laughing, with armloads of blessing" (Psalm 126: 4–6, MSG).

Do you feel that your life is drought-stricken, that you've planted crops of love and faith in vain? You are not alone. The Psalmist of 4,000 years ago felt the same. Yet he dared to ask that God exchange his despair for hurrahs and fill his sinking heart with laughter. Let's agree with him today, boldly marching to the throne of grace to ask the Inventor of Laughter to give us a huge dose.

♥ *From My Heart to Yours: Since God created laughter, the more we chuckle, giggle, and chortle, the more we're following our Heavenly Father's example.*

Chapter 9
How to Talk to Your Pet

If you have pets you know how fun and enlightening a conversation with them can be.

My twenty-pound orange-and-white cat, Rocky, clambers onto the loveseat while I'm reading. His nose nudges my hand. "Meowrrr?" he says.

"What's that, Rocky?"

"Meowrrr?" he says again. He probably thinks I should have listened the first time, and then he wouldn't need to repeat himself.

I scratch his head and force my gaze from the book to see his amber eyes glisten with joy. I once read in a mini-paperback while waiting at the checkout counter that cats hear high tones better than low ones. I want to make sure Rocky knows I care, so I raise my voice three notches.

"What's goin' on today?" I squeak.

"Meow," he says, closing his eyes. Is he disgusted at my Minnie Mouse talk, or is he in kitty heaven?

Just to make sure I switch to my baby-talk tone. "Tell me all about it, Rocks. I know you understand these things."

He purrs and arches his back. Good; it's kitty heaven. "Meow," he answers.

"That's wonderful," I chirp. "I'm so glad to hear it." I return to my book, still petting him in an absentminded fashion. "You are so wise. You amaze me every time we talk."

Dog owners tell me words are unnecessary because their canine pets can read moods and communicate with their eyes and body language. The owner of a pot-bellied pig that's used in therapy claims the little porker can help patients overcome depression. The day of my brother's funeral, my uncle's talking macaw gave me a huge release from my grief by making me laugh until my stomach and face hurt.

I might one day consider owning other types of pets. But I'd hate to lose that unique ability to communicate with my cats in their own language.

♥ *From My Heart to Yours: As a young mother I never allowed anyone to use baby talk with my children. "They need to learn to speak correctly," I preached. But I've noticed I go nuts talking in a silly, high-pitched voice to all my cats. Although I regret my hypocrisy, it sure feels fun to say, "Does Mommy's boy want some milky-wilky?"*

Chapter 10
Meatloaf Wars

When we first married I taught my husband how to create a meatloaf using my mother's recipe. Nothing fancy or unusual, but when it hits your tongue, you're happy to be alive.

I thought I was doing myself a favor by teaching him to cook more entrées than just pork chops and burgers. Aha.

Mister made his first meatloaf. We invited friends over to share it. They mistakenly thought it was his cooking expertise, not my teaching ability or Mom's recipe, that caused their taste buds to tango. *Humph.*

Next time I needed a break from cooking, the new food guru locked himself in the kitchen while he added soy sauce and other secret condiments to "HIS" recipe. More applause from misled tasters disguised as friends.

The final coffin nail for Mom's meatloaf occurred when my hero got up at 5:00 a.m. on the morning he was scheduled to cook, and hand-crumbed the bread as fine as a high note on the violin. That night he grinned to the sides of his chef's hat as my ex-friends helped him devour his masterpiece. When said ex-friends got home, they rushed to their computers and wrote stunning reviews for *Meatloaf for the Stars* magazine and e-mailed Mister, suggesting he start a restaurant.

It's not that I mind never cooking meatloaf again, the shocked stare from Mister when I suggest making Mom's recipe, the guests wondering why all the exotic spices disappeared, the falling of the sky—I can handle all that. It's the demise of Mom's family formula that I grieve. Now it is lost in that huge recipe box in the sky, among 297,685 others from unsuspecting wives who taught their husbands to cook. I hope the angel chefs can keep from embellishing it.

If not, Mom is going to have a thing or two to say when she gets there.

♥ *From My Heart to Yours: If I were emotionally and spiritually mature, I'd be happy that my husband likes to cook. Instead I get miffed when he takes a skill I've taught him and embellishes it, even relishing the applause it brings him. My only comfort is that in heaven we won't be killing animals, so he can't show off his meatloaf-making expertise at my expense!*

Chapter 11
Nevertheless

"Mom, I can quit school now? I already know everything."

I looked down at my son in his baggy shorts and Star Wars T-shirt, the top of his head barely up to my shoulder. I held back a grin. "No, Son, you are not quitting school. You have eight more years to go, then college. Although you're smart you don't know everything."

A storm filled his eyes. "Yes, I do, Mom. I know everything there is to know! So I don't need school anymore."

When he was three and his sister was six, I learned a word that I pulled out whenever the argument started smoking. "*Nevertheless*," I said, "you are not quitting school." He stomped down the hall, slamming the door to his room. This shook our entire 48' x 60' mobile home, rattling every goblet in the built-in hutch. But I stayed glued to my spot in front of the stove, where my spaghetti sauce and I shared a wee chuckle.

After my son came out of his room and got over his pout long enough to eat spaghetti, he eventually went to a university, earned two degrees, and became an animator/writer par excellence. But there were a heckofalotta *neverthelesses* between that pout and those two degrees.

My favorite use of the word was during his junior year of high school. I had pushed him through algebra, dragged him through biology, and prayed him through government class. All he wanted to do was draw cartoons.

"Mom, I will never use any of the stuff they are teaching me. I don't need to know how many bones are in my feet or why we have negative numbers. Animators never use that junk. All I need is art."

"*Nevertheless*, Son, you have to take these classes to get into college to study animation. Those are the hoops you have to jump through. Sorry."

That was fifteen years ago. Last year the animation studio he works for announced the completion of a project they'd done for Microsoft's Halo action comics. This month their city's museum featured the studio's work. When he told me about sitting on the stage with the other animators and fielding interview questions, I let myself grin this time. I patted my word on the back and said, "Good job, *nevertheless*."

♥ *From My Heart to Yours: Apart from marriage, raising kids is the toughest job on the planet, and we can't hope to succeed alone. I'll always be grateful to the Lord for the friend who shared the secret of "nevertheless" with me.*

Chapter 12
Humor and Laughter Quotes

Humor must be vital to our well-being for so many famous people to have commented on it. Here are a few of my favorites.

- "May laughter fill your home, relieve your stress, and strengthen your friendships. Do not let a day go by without laughing. It is good for your health." –Catherine Pulsifer, *Gifts to Give a Friend*

- "Laughter is a tranquilizer with no side effects." –Arnold Glasow

- "Before the assault of laughter, nothing can stand."—Mark Twain

- "Laughter is the shortest distance between two people." –Victor Borge

- "Nobody ever died of laughter." –Sir Max Beerbohm

- "It is impossible for you to be angry and laugh at the same time. Anger and laughter are mutually exclusive and you have the power to choose either." –Dr Wayne W. Dyer

- "Laugh and the world laughs with you; weep and you weep alone." –Ella Wheeler Wilcox

- "Common sense and a sense of humor are the same thing, moving at different speeds. A sense of humor is just common sense, dancing." –William James

- "A man isn't poor if he can still laugh." –Raymond Hitchcock

- "Laughter is a powerful way to tap positive emotions." –Norman Cousins

- "The most wasted of all days is one without laughter." –e.e. cummings

- “A person without a sense of humor is like a wagon without springs. It is jolted by every pebble on the road.”—Henry Ward Beecher

- “Laughter is the sun that drives winter from the face.” –Victor Hugo

- “Always laugh when you can. It is cheap medicine.” –Lord Byron

- “The day is lost in which one has not laughed.” –French proverb

- “Through humor, you can soften some of the worst blows that life delivers. And once you find laughter, no matter how painful your situation might be, you can survive it.” –Bill Cosby

- “Good humor is one of the preservatives of our peace and tranquility.” –Thomas Jefferson

- “Humor is the only test of gravity, and gravity of humor; for a subject which will not bear raillery is suspicious, and a jest which will not bear serious examination is false wit.” –Aristotle

- “Even if there’s nothing to laugh about, laugh on credit.” –Anonymous

- “When people are laughing, they are generally not killing each other.” –Alan Alda

- “We don’t laugh because we’re happy—we’re happy because we laugh.” –William James

- “Humor is the great thing, the saving thing. The minute it crops up, all our irritation and resentment slip away, and a sunny spirit takes their place.” –Mark Twain

❖ "Humor is a serious thing. I like to think of it as one of our greatest natural resources which must be preserved at all costs." –James Thurber

♥ *From My Heart to Yours: I've heard that many comedians and humor writers are prone to depression. Perhaps trying to make their audiences laugh is a way to cheer themselves up.*

Chapter 13
Finger Foods Are for Wimps

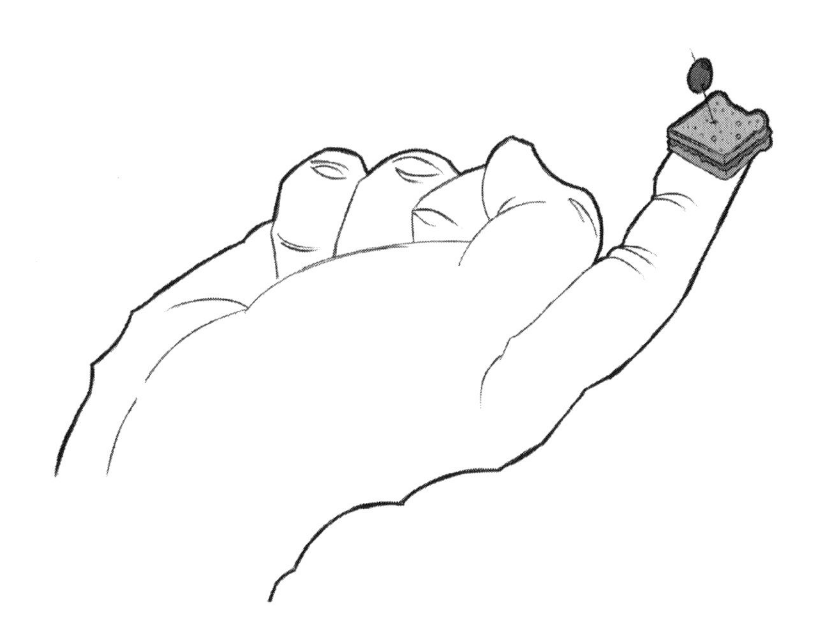

The idea of serving finger foods began innocently enough at a meeting of the Missionary Mamas. Mrs. Practical suggested we bring sandwiches, veggie plates, and fruit skewers to our next church supper instead of the usual noodles, fried chicken, and peach cobblers.

"It will save us preparation time, we won't have to wash silverware, and finger foods are much healthier," she said. Sounded reasonable to our mama ears. We decided to give it a trial run. Little did we imagine we were guillotining the mainstay of our fellowship suppers: recipes handed down from one mama to another, delighting the souls and taste buds of all who partook.

I realize that Nora's homemade noodles contain enough fat to give the Loch Ness monster a coronary, but they glide down your throat ten times smoother than a celery stick with fat-free peanut butter. Betty's ranch-and-bacon cheese ball may make my gallbladder throw a hissy fit, but it entertains my tongue far better than wheat-something squares with cucumber slices cut thinner than my patience. And skewered melon balls just don't zing for me like Tonya's double-chocolate fudge cake.

We ladies used to exchange the best methods for removing coffee stains from upholstery and catch up on family news while we washed casserole dishes and cake pans. Now we just flip the plastic containers from fruit and veggie trays into the trash and wave goodbye. So you see how this whole healthy-finger-food obsession is ruining our deep Christian fellowship.

Yes, I know Jesus served rolls and fish to the crowds. But that was a picnic—centuries before anyone invented green-bean casserole, shepherd's pie, or apple fritters. I'm positive He won't settle for low-fat finger foods at His marriage supper.

> ♥ *From My Heart to Yours: Women's groups can be bastions of comfort and friendship, or battlefields of strife and division. The Lord gave ladies the gift of influence. Although I prefer noodles and chocolate cake to finger foods, I refuse to argue the point. I'd rather use my influence to talk the Missionary Mamas into hosting an old-fashioned potluck dinner.*

Chapter 14

Shopping Queen

I just went in for milk and bread,

I never meant to lose my head,

But by the time I'd reached the door

My cart was dragging on the floor.

"What happened?" cried my shaken spouse,

"You bought enough to fill a house!"

"But Honey, dog food was on sale;

I had to buy the half-price kale;

Here are some socks with rainbow toes,

And polka-dot tissues to blow your nose!

I had to buy snow cones, three for ten,

And chicken livers to feed Uncle Ben,

Who loves to pop in unannounced, you know,

I'll feed him persimmons—just look how they glow!"

I grinned and I gloated, I basked in delight,

That I'd found such bargains for our budget tight.

Did it really matter we didn't have dogs?

Or despised that ol' kale? We'd feed neighbors' hogs!

I guess I'd forgotten poor Uncle Ben's passing,

But fried chicken livers would be such a blessing

At the next carry-in on our fifth-Sunday dinner,

As a shopper, no doubt, I reigned as the winner.

♥ *From my Heart to Yours: This poem was a result of a prompt for a writers' group I belong to. Although I'm less than fond of prompts as a method to get my writing muse working, I ignored my "want to," followed instructions, and got this fun poem as a result. How like our walk with God—when we say, "No!" to our "want to" in order to obey His Word, He rewards us with an abundant life.*

Chapter 15
Ten Rules for the Perfect Pity Party

1. For the perfect pity party, it's important to get upset over something negative that happens to you. Anything will qualify: being unable to get tickets to a concert or a friend forgetting your birthday. Or it could be huge, like a broken engagement or the loss of a job. (Have you noticed the devil isn't fussy when it comes to supplying reasons for a pity party? He knows everyone's special buttons to push).

2. Listen and believe it when Satan says, "You poor, poor thing. You don't deserve to be treated like this. Even Jesus had friends who loved and followed Him." (The Enemy likes to take Scripture and twist it around to make you doubt God's love.)

3. Start feeling sorry for yourself. Believe that no one loves or appreciates you. Do not think of anything or anyone but yourself and your problems. Dwell on the pain until it grows enormous.

4. Call someone you know will sympathize with you and agree you are being mistreated. Do not call anyone who will try to help you see both sides of the issue or who will pray with you. Especially avoid calling someone who gives you an encouraging Scripture or two.

5. Eat like a pig, especially junky foods like cake, brownies, chips, and donuts.

6. Go shopping and buy things you don't need with money you don't have. Credit cards are great for pity parties. Don't listen to your conscience when it tells you this isn't wise. Tell yourself you deserve to be pampered, since you are the only person who cares about you.

7. Don't exercise. Exercise releases endorphins, which combat depression, thus giving you a balanced perspective. The last thing you need at a pity party is logic.

8. Don't visit someone who is worse off than you are or call a friend you know is going through a rough time. That may cause

you to count your blessings, and blessing-counting is not a pity-party game.

9. Don't read the Bible or an uplifting book. Don't listen to Christian music or talk to God. These things are notorious for putting a wet blanket on pity parties.

10. Don't do anything fun that will bring enjoyment to yourself or anyone else. Especially avoid anything that might make you laugh. The goal is to be as miserable as possible, because fun and misery don't mix.

That should about do it for the perfect pity party. Can you tell I've had lots of practice over the years? The only thing I've noticed is that pity parties don't accomplish much except for making me feel worse or making the devil happy. His goal is to steal, kill, and destroy. He wants to steal our joy, kill our relationship with God, and destroy our lives. And I just hate the thought of helping him out by throwing a pity party when I know Jesus came so I could have an overflowing, abundant life (see John 10:10).

♥ *From My Heart to Yours: Attending my own pity parties has been one of the most challenging habits for me to break. I realized the secret is to recognize who sends me the invitation, and to shout "NO!" the minute I'm tempted. Then I kick his sorry self out with praise and thanksgiving.*

Chapter 16
Comedy Movie, Anyone?

Here are the Top Ten Funny Family Movies, according to www.movieguide.org:

1. *My Big Fat Greek Wedding*
2. *The Pink Panther*
3. *Enchanted*
4. *Modern Times* (with Charlie Chaplin)
5. *You Can't Cheat an Honest Man*
6. *It Happened One Night*
7. *The Quiet Man*
8. *Safety Last* (silent film)
9. *Honey, I Blew up the Kid*
10. *Honey, I Shrunk the Kids*

These are the "Top Ten Family-oriented Comedy Films of All Time," according to www.flickechart.com:

1. *The Princess Bride*
2. *Toy Story*
3. *The Gold Rush* (with Charlie Chaplin)
4. *The Goonies*

5. *Wall-E*
6. *Toy Story 2*
7. *Monster, Inc.*
8. *A Christmas Story*
9. *Up*
10. *Toy Story 3*

Do you get the impression that these people have an affinity for Toy Story movies?

Now I wouldn't call my husband a movie nut—more like an organizational genius. At the time of this writing, his movie collection totaled 2,600 films, which he's cataloged in a computer file according to the various cabinets, shelves, and bookcases they live in. If I say, "Let's see a funny movie with a little romance," he goes to his list and picks a few he thinks I'd like. When I choose one he opens a cabinet or goes to a shelf and finds it in minutes. See why I think he's a genius?

These are his favorite funny films:

1. *The Thin Man*
2. *The Shop Around the Corner*
3. *Father Was a Fullback*
4. *You Can't Take It with You*
5. *The Man Who Came to Dinner*

6. *The Court Jester*
7. *Miracle on 34th Street*
8. *The Quiet Man*
9. *Much Ado About Nothing*
10. *Champagne for Caesar*
11. *Christmas in Connecticut*
12. *Sitting Pretty*
13. *The Young in Heart*
14. *Desk Set*
15. *The Canterville Ghost*
16. *Harvey*
17. *The Russians Are Coming*
18. *Donovan's Reef*
19. *Those Magnificent Men in Their Flying Machines*
20. *One, Two, Three*
21. *Father of the Bride*
22. *Adam's Rib*
23. *My Love for Yours*
24. *North to Alaska*
25. *How to Steal a Million*
26. *The Wrong Box*

27. *Teahouse of the August Moon*
28. *Dave*
29. *Roman Holiday*
30. *The 5,000 Fingers of Dr. T.*
31. *No Time for Sergeants*
32. *Holiday*
33. *Sullivan's Travels*
34. *The Inspector General*
35. *Here Come the Nelsons*
36. *The More the Merrier*
37. *Judge Priest*
38. *The Ghost and Mr. Chicken*
39. *Cactus Flower*
40. *Little Giant*

♥ *From My Heart to Yours: Although I'm picky about what movies I watch, I find that losing myself in a comedy film is a tremendous stress-reliever, and much less expensive than a psychiatrist or a trip to the Bahamas. I highly recommend you pick one (or a few) from the above lists and enjoy!*

Chapter 17
The Addict

"Hello. My name is Jeanette. This is my first Nameless Recoverers' meeting." I fidgeted on the cold metal chair, trying to find my voice and my courage in this room full of strangers. Finally I spit out the dreaded words: "I am addicted to Facebook."

No one spoke. A few glanced down at their hands or looked away. *They're embarrassed for me,* I thought. *They are used to druggies, alcoholics, and co-dependents, but Facebook addiction is so stupid.* Nevertheless I plunged ahead.

"It was fun at first, collecting friends from all over the universe. But then I started getting requests to play Karate Kittens and Mafia Mania, which made me late to work. Friends started sending me pillows and bouquets, so I had to reciprocate, didn't I?

"I can't stop poking people, passing out 'Bestie Friend Tags,' and giving thumbs-up to every message on my board. When my husband got up at 2:00 a.m. last night and found me slumped over the bar of dark chocolate (my fix to keep me awake), he told me I needed to join this group. Is there any way can you help me?"

Now it was the leader's turn to fidget. Her face reddened as she struggled to speak.

"I…ah…hmm. Well, Jeanette. We have found that the only way to overcome this type of addiction is to, ahem…"

I leaned forward, anticipating her words of wisdom. She cleared her throat several more times.

At last she continued. "I saw a special on laptops at Circus City last weekend. Perhaps that would motivate your husband to join you on Facebook. You see, I not only lead this Nameless Recoverers' group, I also serve as the International Facebook facilitator. If you'll give me your full name, I'll *friend* you the minute I get home tonight."

♥ *From My Heart to Yours: Although I enjoy social networking and am convinced Jesus would use it to market His message if He walked the earth today, I have to be careful I don't let it become a tyrant instead of a tool. I'm determined that my only addiction be Jesus.*

Chapter 18
Teaching: Not for the Faint of Heart

My palms were sweating as I realized I had serious car trouble. *I've got to get this car to the median*, I thought, looking over my shoulder at three lanes of early morning L.A. traffic. *I need a miracle like the parting of the Red Sea.* Wait, wrong Bible story. This was December 20. How about a miracle similar to finding a birthing manger in Bethlehem? *Whatever! Just help me get to school on time, Lord.*

It was the last day of school before Christmas vacation. My students had always been generous in past years, but I knew they'd pour on the presents today, since it was my final year teaching at the small private school my own kids attended. We were about to move across the country.

I wasn't fretting over leaving my teens at home alone while I dashed my husband to the train station, or worried about the expense of fixing whatever troubled our sick car. I was thinking of those beribboned boxes of stationery I'd re-gift at the next Missionary Mamas Christmas party, the "Best Teacher" mugs I'd drink from twice before giving them to Goodwill, and the matching sets of dishtowels I'd put in a drawer to give my kids' teachers next Christmas. The thought of missing all that loot made me want to cry.

I shot up my favorite prayer: "Lord, help me, please!"

As I put the car in neutral, opened the door so I could step out, and started to push, a pickup truck pulled up behind me. The driver motioned me to get back in so he could push me from behind. I was able to turn the corner and ease the car to a stop. I smiled as I waved my thanks to the kind driver, noticing the embroidered name on his blue uniform: ***CLARENCE***. *"Thanks, Lord,"* I chuckled, recalling the angel character from the classic Christmas film *It's a Wonderful Life.* I listened for the telltale bell to ring, wondering if he'd just earned his wings.

By the time I jogged the quarter-mile home, more than my palms were sweating, but I didn't have time to change clothes. Those gifts were waiting.

My sixteen-year-old daughter was thrilled that she got to drive us to school in her car. Her younger brother was not amused. "Mom, the last time she drove, she went the wrong way up a one-way street and nearly killed us!"

"We'll just have to risk it, Son. I may never have another bonanza like this again. I have to get while the getting is good." He sighed and grabbed two overstuffed pillows from the couch on his way out the door. (This was the dark ages, before airbags.)

We made it to school in record time with only one mishap—a scratch on the passenger side from a holly bush in a residential neighborhood. "That's okay, Honey," I crooned to my daring young driver. "It's hard to judge your speed when you're turning corners. Those people shouldn't have planted that bush so close to the sidewalk."

As my son staggered out of the backseat, still clutching his pillows, he moaned and slapped his forehead. "We forgot our lunches, Mom. You made us leave in such a hurry that we left them on the kitchen table. I can't make it till 3:30 with nothing to eat!"

I put my arm around his shoulder as we walked into the building together. "Don't worry, Son. I'm counting on at least three boxes of See's candy and two fruitcakes. I'll share with you, okay?"

♥ *From My Heart to Yours: I hate to think I was having a fit of greed that historical December day; I prefer to think I was giving my students the opportunity to bless me, so the Lord in turn could bless them. After all, it's not cool at their age to say, "You're a fabulous teacher, Mrs. L." But it's fine to bring me gifts. And who am I to stand in the way of a little teenage appreciation?*

Chapter 19
An Outhouse to Celebrate

"Did you see that?" my husband guffawed, pointing out the car window on a recent road trip.

"No, what was it?" I said.

"A billboard for an Outhouse Festival. I can't believe it!"

By now I was giggling too. "What is there to celebrate about outhouses?"

I understand celebrating honeybees, covered bridges, and Raggedy Ann & Andy. Bring on the parades! Sell deep-fried Twinkies and corn dogs. Hire a brass band to play on the town square.

But outhouses? Every time I must use one, I'm not thinking of ponies, trombones, or yummy junk food.

I suppose an outhouse is a great invention if you're in the middle of Nowheresville and can't find a bush to hide behind. But to have an entire weekend dedicated to holes and the houses that hide them? How desperate must you be for something to party over?

If you really want to celebrate, I have a few ideas for you:

❖ Celebrate living in a nation where you have a free education, can criticize a political candidate without being arrested, and can worship whatever deity you choose.

❖ Even if you have only one set of clothes and enough food for today, celebrate being rich. Most dogs and cats in this country live better than millions of people in the rest of the world.

❖ If you can read this article, celebrate that you possess a sound mind and healthy eyes.

❖ Celebrate a God who gave you all the wonder of creation for your enjoyment, and who loves you just as you are.

I'll bet you can come up with a few more reasons to celebrate, things we fail to appreciate until we're without them. For that matter, next time I go camping, I may have to reconsider celebrating an outhouse after all.

♥ *From My Heart to Yours: We rarely appreciate a convenience until we're forced to do without it. To add some joy to your day, try thanking God for every little invention you use that makes your life easier.*

Chapter 20
You Are Smarter Than You Think!

Wanna feel extra smart today? Look at these five ditzy doings:

Who Needs Some Change?

When the bill at a drive-in burger shop came to $4.25, Aunt Minnie handed the young cashier a $5-bill and a quarter. The teenager gazed at the money for a moment then said, "You gave me too much."

"I know," Aunt Minnie replied. "This way you give me an even dollar in change."

The cashier left the window and soon returned with the manager. "I'm sorry, ma'am; we can't do this type of thing," the manager said.

Aunt Minnie shrugged as the teenager handed her $1.75 in change.

Stop Endangering the Deer

A rural newspaper received this letter from a concerned reader: "I think the Township needs to move the Deer Crossing sign out on Highway 14. Too many deer are getting hit and killed there. They need a safer place to cross."

Hardworking Mechanic

When a lady went to the mechanic's shop to pick up her car after a repair, the mechanic apologized for locking the keys inside. He was busy finagling to get the door on the driver's side open. The lady walked around to the passenger side. Finding it unlocked she opened the door then said to the mechanic, "Hey, this side is unlocked."

"I know," he replied, "I already managed to get that side opened."

Advice for Wannabe Bank Robbers

If you plan to rob a bank, be careful where you write your hold-up note. One robber put his on the back of a deposit slip—his own!

Battery Heat

Believe it or not I have been guilty of a few dumb doings myself. While in the lunchroom at a former job, I noticed the clock had stopped. I called the facilities manager to bring some batteries the next time he came down to the kitchen. A few minutes later he showed up, batteries in hand.

"Jeanette," he said, "this clock is electric; the cord is hanging right here." He plugged it in and set the time. Heat crept up my neck and into my face as I said, "Well, the cord and wall are both white. It blended in!"

♥ *From My Heart to Yours: How refreshing to discover that we're not the only ones who sometimes act silly. We enjoy hearing about others' slip-ups. It gives us hope that if they can manage life in their mental condition, surely we can, too.*

Chapter 21
Three Heads

"Wow, we found that quickly by working together," I told my co-worker Jolene. "Just proves that three heads are better than one!"

"Yes, but I count only two of us here, Jeanette."

I doubled over with laughter when I realized how I'd changed that wise old saying. When I told my husband about my blunder, I laughed even harder.

My giggles dripped onto him, and he smiled as big as a watermelon slice. "It's good that you can laugh at yourself," he said.

"Well, why not? It beats feeling embarrassed by the stupid things I do. Everyone gets discombobulated from time to time. Why should I be exempt from making an idiot of myself? If I can laugh about my flubs, other people around me feel more comfortable. Then when they make mistakes, they won't be so self-conscious. They see I'm as real as they are, even though I'm a preacher's wife. Perhaps when they have a problem that seems overwhelming, they'll feel comfortable confiding in me because they've witnessed one of my weak moments."

There is nothing to gain from pretending to be perfect. We only fool ourselves when we act as if the dumb things we do are someone else's fault, we meant to do them, or we can't help ourselves. That's called pride, and the word "pride" has a big fat "I" in the middle of it, not to mention that the Bible says God hates it.

Laughing at ourselves is a way of loving ourselves, of showing we're comfortable with the person God made us, imperfections and all. So go ahead. Next time you do or say something crazy—and it probably won't be too long from now—get free and laugh at yourself. We'll like you better, and so will you!

♥ *From My Heart to Yours: Some people look at me funny when I tell them about the ditzy things I do. But I figure I'm doing the world a favor. If I can make you shake your head when I can't remember the word for* milk, *you won't feel so horrible the next time you call one of your kids the dog's name.*

Chapter 22
The Snake Skedaddle

Grandma Viola never hid her aversion for snakes, but her spunky way of eradicating them shocked me.

I discovered her system when my husband and I visited her and Granddad in their new home that overlooked a juniper-covered hillside in a suburb of San Diego, California. While Granddad puttered at the barbeque, we chatted with Grandma. In the midst of a conversation about neighbors and gas prices, she suddenly lowered her voice to the gold shag carpet. "Don't tell your granddad, but I killed a snake in the backyard last week."

My mouth popped open. "Grandma! You what?"

"Yep," she said. "As soon as I saw that hissing, yellow-eyed demon, I ran to the garage and grabbed a shovel. I beat that rascal to death. Then I picked up its body with the shovel handle and threw it over the hillside. If your granddad found out, he'd move us back to L.A. So you keep quiet, okay?"

Still in shock I nodded, but I had to ask, "Was that the first snake you've seen since you moved here?"

Grandma chuckled. "Oh no, that was the fourth one. I always do them the same way—beat the bajeebers out of 'em, then toss 'em over the hillside. I hate snakes. They scare me to kingdom come. Do you kids want some more coffee?" And off she headed for the kitchen.

That was over three decades ago, and I'm still shaking my head at Grandma's moxie. All the snakes I've met laugh at my screams when I encounter their slithering selves. "You're no relation to Viola Tomson," they mock. "The stories we've heard of her shovel-beatings make our skin crawl. How can you call yourself her granddaughter?"

"I inherited Granddad's genes," I holler, skedaddling away. "Grandma faced her fear with a shovel; Granddad moved!"

♥ *From My Heart to Yours: Jesus had more than one method of overcoming danger. When a mega-storm threatened to drown Him and His friends, He spoke to it. When jealous religious leaders wanted to throw Him over a cliff, He walked away. Neither method is godlier than the other. Let His spirit lead you in each instance.*

Chapter 23
It's a Small(er) World

While eating baby-back ribs recently, I noticed how dinner napkins are shrinking. It's bad enough that manufacturers inject air into the napkins to make them appear plump; now they're decreasing their size. One used to cover my whole lap; these days it barely fits on the top third of a thigh.

Candy bars have also been shrinking with the times. Years ago it took me five bites to eat my Gooey-Wooey bar. Today I have to get out Grandma's magnifying glass to gaze at its loveliness before I down it in two nibbles.

And have you been as shocked as I have about how ice-cream containers dwindled overnight from half a gallon to one and a half quarts? We used to serve ice cream with our birthday cakes. Nowadays we simply wave the carton over each plate as a sweet remembrance of more generous times.

Coffee-can shrinkage is another travesty. Remember when you bought coffee by the pound? These days it comes in 12- or 13-oz. packages—for the same price as before. Soon they'll be selling it by the cup and charging $3.50 a slurp. Oh, that's right; they're already doing that.

TV shows now take up only forty-five minutes instead of fifty-two. Today's cars are the size of my grandson's scooter. Even Band-Aids barely cover a boo-boo anymore.

I'm so relieved that Jesus' love never shrinks or diminishes in strength. Jesus stays the same year after year, century after century, forever—even if my favorite pants shrink to the size of a dinner napkin.

♥ *From My Heart to Yours: Although I tend to base the worth of an item on its size, that doesn't matter when it comes to problems. God is bigger than any or all of them. Next time one threatens to steal my joy, I need to remind myself of the huge, powerful hand of my Father.*

Chapter 24
Nine Ways Humor Helps

According to Dr. Paul E. McGhee in his book *Health, Healing, and the Amuse System,* humor helps:

1. **Strengthen our immune system** by increasing immunoglobulin A, which protects us against colds and flu

2. **Increase T-cells**, which hunt down and destroy tumor cells, foreign organisms, and viruses

3. **Curb food cravings**

4. **Increase our tolerance for and reduce pain**

5. **Decrease levels of stress hormones**

6. **Lower blood pressure**

In "Effectiveness of the Use of Humor on Persuasive Messages in Print," James N. Watkins cites university studies that claimed humor:

7. **Doubles the persuasiveness of a message**

8. **Increases comprehension in learning**

9. **Makes us smarter**[i]

♥ *From My Heart to Yours: Although here I cited only two sources for proof that humor helps us thrive emotionally and physically, you can find hundreds—possibly thousands—of books and articles to support what God said through the writer of Proverbs:* "A cheerful disposition is good for your health; gloom and doom leave you bone-tired" (Proverbs 17:22 MSG).

Chapter 25
If Socks Could Talk

What is it with socks? Do you think they conspire to separate when we wash them? Perhaps as they come off the assembly line and their price tags are attached, they yell to each other, "See you the first week in November at the International Sock Reunion. This year we meet in St. Louis!"

For the first few months you own them, they behave, staying in tidy pairs from the hamper to the dryer. But soon the time approaches for their annual get-together with the friends they haven't seen since birth. They start to strategize in the drawer at night.

"Hey, Bernie, you drop on the floor when the guy throws you in the hamper from across the bedroom. You know how he likes to pretend he's Michael Jordan. Scrunch behind the dresser where no one will find you. I'll fall out of the lady's hand when she tosses clothes into the washer. We'll meet outside at ten tomorrow night and hitchhike to St. Louis. I can't wait to see if one of those little French anklets with the purple lace around their cuffs shows up."

In the meantime the orphaned socks slump in the back of the bottom drawer, reading the novel *Left Behind* and wondering what they did wrong. A men's trouser sock grumbles to an athletic, "They better find my mate soon; I haven't been outta this drawer since last October. I just hope the sock police didn't catch him. Their toe-jam torture nearly ruined my sister's boy. I heard the black dress shoe telling its mate how he could hardly breathe after a day with my nephew."

"I don't believe you," cries the athletic sock, huffing in disgust. "What kind of idiot do you think I am? Everyone knows shoes can't talk!"

♥ *From My Heart to Yours: I love the story in the Bible about the talking donkey God used to rebuke a prophet gone astray. Makes me want to obey the Lord's direction for my life, or He might decide to make one of my socks talk to me when I've wandered off His path.*

Chapter 26
The Way We Were

Dear Granddaughter:

Since you asked about "the olden days," I thought you'd enjoy a written account of the primitive conditions in which Grandpa and I grew up.

Facebook hadn't been invented back then, so meeting people and making friends was a complicated process. It involved rituals like talking to people, shaking their hands, and asking them questions about their interests.

We lowered and raised our car windows by cranking handles

attached to the inside doors of the cars. We unlocked the car doors with keys and then had to lock them by pushing a button down by hand!

Garage doors could only be opened and closed manually, using a handle on the front. We had to get out of the car, walk to the garage, and open or close it ourselves.

TVs in the dark ages had no remote controls. We got up from the couch and walked across the room to change the channel or turn the volume down with a knob attached to the front of the TV set. We had no *couch potatoes* in those days, either.

When we used telephones we had to dial the other person by poking our finger into holes in a numbered plastic circle on the front of the phone. We even *talked* to the person on the other end. In those days a *text* referred to a book we used for schoolwork.

We also sent messages to friends with items called *letters*, written with devices named *pens,* on sheets of paper, and we put them in a blue box on a street corner. They were sorted and sent in a truck to our friends' houses. Sometimes they took days to arrive!

I know this has shocked you, and you're amazed that we survived. But people in the olden days were tougher. Without Facebook, remotes, and texting, we had to be.

With love,

Your Savvy Grandma

♥ *From My Heart to Yours: I think every generation looks back on earlier days and imagines the past was simpler and sweeter. We can find contentment in spite of changes that happen faster than a weed sprouts. Just keep a kid handy to explain things!*

Chapter 27
The Lead-Footed Driver Award

While navigating busy Los Angeles streets, my mother often said, "Just look at that Jehu, running through a stop sign," or, "He drives like a Jehu!" As a child, I wondered what sort of creature a "Jehu" was. Then I discovered his story in the Bible.

Jehu served as a captain in the Israelite army during the reign of the evil king Joram. After Elisha's servant anointed Jehu as king to replace Joram, Jehu jumped into his chariot and drove to Jezreel to overthrow the sitting king. One of Joram's tower watchmen recognized Jehu while he was still afar off. From the vibrant color of his chariot? From his stunning horses? From his long, shiny hair flowing in the wind? No.

The watchman recognized Jehu's reckless driving because the army captain was known throughout the land for his attraction to fast wheels!

"So the watchman reported saying, "He went up to them and is not coming back; and the driving is like the driving of Jehu the son of Nimshi, for he drives furiously!"(2 Kings 9:20, NKJV).

While in Jezreel, Jehu became a hero by slaughtering Joram and then ridding the land of Joram's wicked mother, Jezebel (No, he didn't run over her.)

Are you ever tempted to think God can't use you to accomplish anything greater than singing in the choir or cooking a roast for the next potluck? Do you long to soar like an eagle but feel like you're stuck with a flock of turkeys? You may wonder why God gives all the exciting jobs and sparkly personalities to others. But wait!

Before you despair, remember Jehu.

He wasn't a prophet who multiplied oil for starving widows or healed lepers, and he wasn't an author who changed the course of history with his bestselling book. Jehu was an ordinary man whom God used to accomplish mighty, heroic deeds. His only talent was his crazy driving.

Now don't you suppose the same Lord who took a Jehu and made him into a hero can cause your life to count for a special purpose? Makes you want to stay in the race for a few more miles to see what God will do through you, doesn't it?

♥ *From My Heart to Yours: I find it amusing that the lead-footed-driver award goes to a man. History continues to repeat itself century after century….*

Chapter 28
Got Pain? Laugh it Away

Wait just a minute. Can you really control pain by laughing? That seems too simple.

Robin Dunbar, a study researcher at the University of Oxford, and several of his colleagues set out to determine if the endorphin rush that laughter provides increases our tolerance for pain. They tested study participants for their pain tolerance, exposed them to both control and laughter-inducing tests, and then measured pain levels again. The result? "Across all tests, the participants' ability to tolerate pain jumped after laughing."

From an article on justlaughter.com, medical experts in the United States found that laughter helped children relax, which had a major impact on how they dealt with and accepted pain.

The researchers believe the healing power of humor can reduce pain and stimulate the immune function in children with cancer, diabetes, or AIDS, as well as in children receiving organ transplants and bone marrow treatments.

Dr. Margaret Stuber, who led the research, said, "We think laughter could be used to help children who are undergoing painful procedures or who suffer from pain-expectation anxiety. In the future, patients watching humorous videos could become a standard component of some medical procedures."

The US study, Rx Laughter, is a collaboration between the entertainment industry, pediatrics, and psychiatry. They asked twenty-one children, aged eight to fourteen, to put their hand into cold water and found the whole group tolerated the temperature longer while watching a funny video.

Those who laughed most remembered less of the pain, and hormone tests on their saliva showed their stress levels were lower after laughing.

My friend Beth proved this in her own life when giving birth to her first baby (the ultimate test of pain tolerance). "They wouldn't let me push yet," she said, "but the pain was unbearable. Then my husband turned on the TV and found a funny movie. As long as I was laughing, the labor pains didn't feel half as intense. Miraculously, when the credits at the end of the movie rolled on the screen, the nurse said, 'You can push now.' I later told my husband, 'Next time we have a baby, we're gonna come prepared with the funniest movies we can find to get us through labor!'"

♥ *From My Heart to Yours: I don't recommend having a baby to test if laughter increases your tolerance for pain. But it couldn't hurt to pop in a funny movie or hang out with a goofy friend next time you twist your ankle or stub your toe.*

Chapter 29
From Grossly Green to Sparkling Clean

When Kevin bought the monster-size bottle of Grossly Green mouthwash, I wondered if we'd live long enough to use it up—or die trying. Whoever invented the formula for this stuff must have taste buds of steel, or they concocted it in hopes that each of their least favorite politicians would buy a case and gag to death.

Each time I gargled was a great excuse to chase it with a bowl of ice cream or a Hershey's Special Dark® candy bar. But that worked for only a few weeks. It's not worth a completely new wardrobe two sizes bigger just to have lovely breath.

We can't throw the mouthwash out; we've invested half a week's salary in it. Those large economy sizes require the kinds of bills with unknown presidents' faces on them. We could invite friends over and serve them garlic fettuccini, garlic bread, and garlic cookies for dessert, then say, "Oops, look what we did," and then offer them a huge aperitif of Grossly Green. But we'd run out of friends before the bottle was empty.

I discovered the answer to our dilemma while preparing for church one morning in the back bathroom. I noticed a ring in the toilet, so I rummaged for some cleanser or toilet bowl goop. I was already running late, and all I could find under the sink was half a bottle of Grossly Green. Aha! No self-respecting toilet would dare stay dirty after a few swishes of this bright chartreuse poison. In fact, the scream of horror from the toilet as I swished gave me a hint that it will never again get a ring for fear I'd repeat the torture.

Kev may wonder why the Grossly Green is disappearing so fast. I'm sure he was expecting it to last a decade or more. If he mentions it I'll just point to our sparkling, whimpering toilet and tell him that his bargain of the century works better as a bowl cleaner than its original intended use.

♥ *From My Heart to Yours: One of my greatest reliefs upon entering heaven will be the lack of needing to clean. No dirt, dust, grime, or toilet rings there. In fact, no need for toilets at all. Ah, glory!*

Chapter 30
Hotel-Room Follies

The way airlines charge for every amenity from pillows to baggage, I wonder how soon hotels will follow suit. I can only imagine…

When we check into our favorite hotel, the calm-as-a-tortoise owner says, "Would you like to rent some towels, Mr. and Mrs. Levellie?" Although I won the Talkathon USA contest ten years in a row and my husband is a preacher, we are both speechless.

"What do you mean, rent towels? We've stayed here for the last five years whenever we visit our daughter and her family. You've never charged for towels before."

He smiles, feigning patience. "It's our new system. Vandalism was so high that our general manager required us to charge for towels. But if you'd rather not do that, you can use the body-sized blow dryer we've installed in all the bathrooms. Many of our guests prefer it."

My face turns four shades of crimson as I imagine myself standing in front of a huge blow dryer, body fat jiggling at seventy-five mph. "No, thank you," I say. "We'll borrow some Dora the Explorer and Bob the Builder towels from our daughter. Any other changes we should know about?"

"Oh, yes." He grins. "We've replaced the mini-steam irons with full-sized irons."

"Great," says my husband. "Last time it took Jeanette forty minutes to iron my shirt with that little Barbie-sized iron and ironing board you gave us."

The owner looks sympathetic. "Well, I think you'll find this iron much faster. But be careful when you use it; the chain is only a foot long."

"Chain?" I howl.

"Yes, we can't have them stolen like the towels. We chain them to the ironing boards."

I sigh as I pick up our room key and turn to my husband. "At least we have a bed to sleep in, Honey."

"Oh, you want a bed?" says the owner, eyebrows rising. "That will be an extra forty dollars, please."

♥ *From My Heart to Yours: Whenever we stay in a hotel room, I check the desk drawer to make sure there's a Gideon Bible in it. My stepdad, who changed from an ornery sinner to a loving saint when he met Jesus, spent the last thirty years of his life as a Gideon. One of the few times I saw him cry was when he told stories of sharing the Word of God and the transformations that took place because of the gospel.*

Chapter 31
Perfectly Silly

Go lie down on the bed; I want to tell you something. Although I've never heard an audible voice from the Lord, His insistent call to my heart was impossible to ignore.

"Right now, Lord? I'm in the middle of cleaning house and still have a hundred things to finish before Adrienne and Carol arrive. Can't you speak to me while I mop the floor?"

No. You need to be still in order to hear this.

"Oh, all right." I gritted my teeth as I rushed to the bedroom and plopped on the bed. I found it difficult to listen when cobwebs taunted me from the ceiling. I squeezed my eyes shut.

"What is it, Lord?" I grumbled, wanting to rush through this conversation so I could finish mopping. As usual I'd dawdled all week, then tornadoed through Saturday to scrub and shine. It wasn't the Lord's fault, but I blamed Him anyway. He had interrupted my plan.

"Jeanette, you are trying too hard to impress people with your perfection. You're not fooling anyone. By the time Adrienne and Carol get here, you'll be an exhausted mess."

"But Lord, You are perfect, and the Word says to imitate You."

Yes, but I am not a perfectionist. I'm too realistic to think you or anyone else will ever be flawless in this life. You frustrate yourself when you strive to make no mistakes or try to give the impression of flawlessness. My job is to be perfect. Your imitation of Me should be to love others. Pretending you never fail, at housework or any venture, is not love. It's unreality.

"Okay, Lord. I see I'm acting silly, not trusting You to help me clean my house, trying too hard to impress my friends. I repent. Thanks for the correction." As I bounded off the bed to return to my mop, I heard His final words:

Any time.

I'd like to tell you this interchange took place last week. It was closer to twenty years ago. I still wrestle more than I should with striving to look perfect. And I still end up frustrated.

When Jesus came and laid down His life for us, He knew beforehand that we'd not behave perfectly after we got saved. He came anyway, reconciling us to God while we were still sinners. His perfect sacrifice was the only way to bring us into God's family.

All our striving to look faultless adds nothing to His gift of salvation. We simply accept His gift and enter into fellowship with Him.

This isn't an excuse to act lazy or to willfully sin, saying, "Oh well, that's why Jesus died. He knows I'm not perfect." But neither is it an excuse to pretend to be something we're not.

When we pretend to be flawless, we don't impress God or anyone else. It's okay to say, "Oops. That was stupid of me. I apologize." In fact, it endears us to others when we let down our masks and admit we are still in the "rough draft" stage. People feel more comfortable around us when we let them know we're aware we have faults. Then when we tell them about Jesus, they'll be more likely to listen.

♥ *From My Heart to Yours: Someday I'll be perfect. So will you if you belong to Jesus. Until then let's quit looking silly by trying to appear perfect. Let's be real.*

Chapter 32
Comical Signs: Find Them and Laugh

Have you heard of Jeff Deck and Benjamin Herson's Typo Eradication Advancement League (TEAL)? It's a campaign they've launched to correct spelling and grammar mistakes on American signs. Jeff and Ben found one of the best—or worst—examples on the Desert View Watchtower at the Grand Canyon, where the sign promises: "emense westward view of the Grand Canyon."

Instead of admitting their blunder, officials put a spin on the mistake by claiming "a unique historical object of irreplaceable value." And they weren't talking about the Grand Canyon—they were defending the spelling of *emense.*

To add rudeness to their conceit, officials charged Deck and Herson with vandalism for trying to correct the spelling error on the sign. They were fined $3,035 and banned from national parks for a year.

"We're not going after people in a self-righteous manner, like fashion police. Or trying to make them look stupid," Deck said. "Instead, we're addressing specific errors like confusing 'its' for 'it's' or 'you're' for 'your.' Finding and correcting these, even every once in a while, is incredibly satisfying."

To date Jeff and Benjamin have identified 231 signs with spelling or punctuation mistakes. I think they might have missed the following…

❖On a Maine shop: "Our goal is to give our customers the lowest possible prices and workmanship."

❖In the office of a loan company: "Ask about our plans for owning your home."

❖In a New York coffee shop: "Customers who consider our waitress rude should see the manager."

❖Near a diner/gas station in Indiana: "Eat here and get gas."

❖In the window of a Kentucky appliance store: "Don't kill your wife. Let our washing machine do the dirty work."

❖On a sign at an anti-gambling rally: "Teach our Children Reading, Writing, and *Arithetic*, not Gambling."

❖On the lawn of a school: "School of Nursing and Midwifery: Deliveries at Rear of Building."

❖On a mall maintenance shop: "We can repair anything. Please knock hard on the door; the bell doesn't work."

❖Warning sign at a beach: "Beyond this point you may encounter nude sunbathers eating waffles."

❖In an elevator: "Customers should use push buttons to open automatic doors."

♥ *From My Heart to Yours: I'm sure that those who made these blunders could never guess how many people are laughing at them. But they might be delighted if they knew the enormous entertainment value their silly signs provide.*

Chapter 33
In this Corner...Kangaroos

Not all women have it. A few of us were still asleep the morning they handed out the I-love-housework gene.

"Dust bunnies are for wimps" became my motto when I discovered dust kangaroos, with families of dust joeys springing out of their pockets every few days to stir up some fun.

Because we live in the parsonage and my husband's desk is a pulpit, I figure I should try to appear neat once or twice a year. So I give myself a major motivation to clean house by inviting guests to dinner.

The only problem with this clever plan is that I wait until the day of the party to start my cleaning mania. I race around the dining table disrobing chair backs of their sweaters and flinging them into shocked closets. The windowsills resent my removal of the dust that's kept them warm for the last six weeks. My kitchen floor gets tipsy on Spic 'n' Span.

After the guests leave I flop on the couch and moan. "Why do I torture myself like this? What possessed me to invite seventeen people over? Well, at least the house looks sparkly. Let's keep it this way forever!" I know I am duping no one but myself. It's as realistic as stating, "I will never overreact again."

The only time I enjoyed housework was when we were first married and the pride of reigning as queen over my own domain spurred me to dust, mop, and scrub. That cleaning frenzy lasted two whole weeks. After that I concocted my brilliant invite-friends-over scheme.

Once we had kids I began worrying: What if they asked their kindergarten teacher what a dustpan was? To avoid this embarrassment I gave them chores at very early ages. But we had to hold off when our daughter whipped a sewing kit out of her pocket and offered to mend the ripped jeans the adult helper in her preschool class was wearing.

When our kids were eight and eleven, we took them to a discount store and let them pick out their own laundry baskets. On the way home I casually said, "Guess what we're doing today. I'm going to teach you to wash clothes."

From the rearview mirror I caught sight of our daughter rolling her eyes as she said, "I knew there had to be a catch!"

"Someday you'll thank me," I said.

As teenagers our kids did all the cleaning except changing the sheets on our bed. It worked beautifully. Until our daughter moved to college and my son and I divided her chores between us. He got his done all right, since I raised his salary two dollars a week. But mine…well. I always have had a fondness for baby kangaroos.

♥ *From My Heart to Yours: Some people actually enjoy cleaning; can you believe it? It's their gift from the Lord, and I'm more than happy to pay them for exercising it in my home!*

Chapter 34
Maggie Moments

My husband met me at the door, his eyebrows in upside-down-V formation. Two signs of major worry. "Is everything okay, Hon? You just went to mail one dinky package."

I threw my purse and myself onto the couch, sighing louder than usual. "I had a Maggie moment," I huffed.

He shook his head and grinned. A look of relaxed understanding replaced the V-formation.

Maggie, bless her darling heart and ditzy head, is a crisis magnet. She's the one person in our family we can rely on to add major doses of drama to our lives. Every errand turns into a screenplay for a feature film.

Tag along with Maggie as she takes a recent trip to the market for a bag of noodles.

"I think it was that checker's first day on the job," Maggie moaned, dumping her sack of groceries on the kitchen counter. "She didn't know where the noodles were and had to call the manager. He showed me the correct aisle, but they were out of whole-wheat noodles. So I decided to run up to the Pine Street Market. That took forever since I got behind a funeral procession, and then I discovered the store had gone out of business. I had to go back to the first market and buy flour and eggs to make our own noodles. It'll only take three hours. You don't mind having dinner a little late tonight, do you?"

We've tried to analyze why Maggie thrives on trouble. We can go to the post office, market, or bank, and run into glitches that annoy us to Mars and back. Yet we manage to get only a tenth of the emotional surge from our episodes that Maggie receives. We still haven't figured out why her predicaments are superior to ours.

But hey, maybe you can you help us. I see by your knowing smile that you have a Maggie in your family too.

♥ *From My Heart to Yours: People who complicate everything from breakfast to buying stamps must need excitement in their lives. Or they feel insignificant and unnoticed. We don't giggle behind their backs to mock them; it's just our way of coping with their quirks. I think it might help them manage life better if we added a prayer for them after our parodies.*

Chapter 35
Tomorrow's Special: Frog Legs

Frogs in every windowsill. Frogs in all the cupboards and mixing bowls. Frogs in every bed, from the king's silken sheets to the servant's coarse floor mats. The entire land of Egypt was hopping with frogs!

This second plague that was inflicted on Israel's captors, the Egyptians, seemed to bring Pharaoh to his senses. When he summoned Moses, asking that he entreat the Lord for a divine frog disposal, Pharaoh even promised to release the Israelites.

Moses nodded. "Okay. When shall I ask God to remove the frogs?" Here are his exact words:

> "The honor is yours to tell me: when shall I entreat for you and your servants and your people, that the frogs be destroyed from you and your houses, that they may be left only in the Nile?"
>
> Then he said, "Tomorrow." So he said, "May it be according to your word, that you may know that there is no one like the LORD our God" (Exodus 8: 9–10, NASB).

Are you thinking what I'm thinking? *Why wouldn't Pharaoh ask for immediate relief from his amphibian anguish? Why spend one more night—even one more hour—buried in frogs?*

But before I judge old Pharaoh too harshly, I must recall the times God has convicted me of a sin, offering me immediate forgiveness through His Son, Jesus. Did I freely give up the pride, gossip, and bitterness plaguing me? Or did I tell the Lord to come back in the morning, so I could eat just one more meal with the frogs?

Perhaps I can learn from Pharaoh's foolishness. May I change that "tomorrow" to "right now," Lord?

♥ *From My Heart to Yours: God will let us keep our bad habits one more day or month or year. But His love always comes to our rescue the minute we're willing to let go.*

Chapter 36
Ten Ways to Help Yourself Laugh

Most of us think we can't force ourselves to laugh, that funny things must happen to us or around us to bring on the chuckles. But we can put ourselves in situations where laughter is more likely. Here are a few ideas.

1. **Spend time with fun, lighthearted people.** People who laugh readily, both at themselves and at life's absurdities, and who routinely find the humor in everyday events will add joy to your life. Their playful point of view is contagious.

2. **Watch YouTube videos of bloopers** or funny pets and/or kids

3. **When you hear laughter, seek it out.** Ask, "What's so funny?" People are usually happy to share something humorous because it gives them an opportunity feed off the humor you find in it, which starts the hilarity all over again.

4. **Play with a kid.** Have you noticed that children laugh ten times more than adults? Discover what makes them laugh, and do it with them.

5. **Exaggerate a frustrating situation to a friend.** Use enormous gestures, a loud voice, and sarcasm to act out the ridiculous. Play all the parts to see how ridiculous you can make it seem.

6. **Check out the humor section** in your library or bookstore.

7. **Go to a comedy club** with a friend. Sharing a funny experience makes it more enjoyable, and you're more likely to laugh if someone beside you is also amused.

8. **Watch a funny movie or TV show**, especially with someone who laughs easily and shares your sense of humor.

9. **Read a book of jokes**, look at a humor website, or read the newspaper comics.

10. **Bring humor into conversations.** Ask people, "What's the funniest thing that happened to you today? This week? In your life?"

♥ *From My Heart to Yours: I have sometimes prayed that God would give us more laughter in our day. Since I believe it delights the Lord to answer such a prayer, I then envision myself and whoever I'm with laughing together.*

Chapter 37
Mall in a Pocket

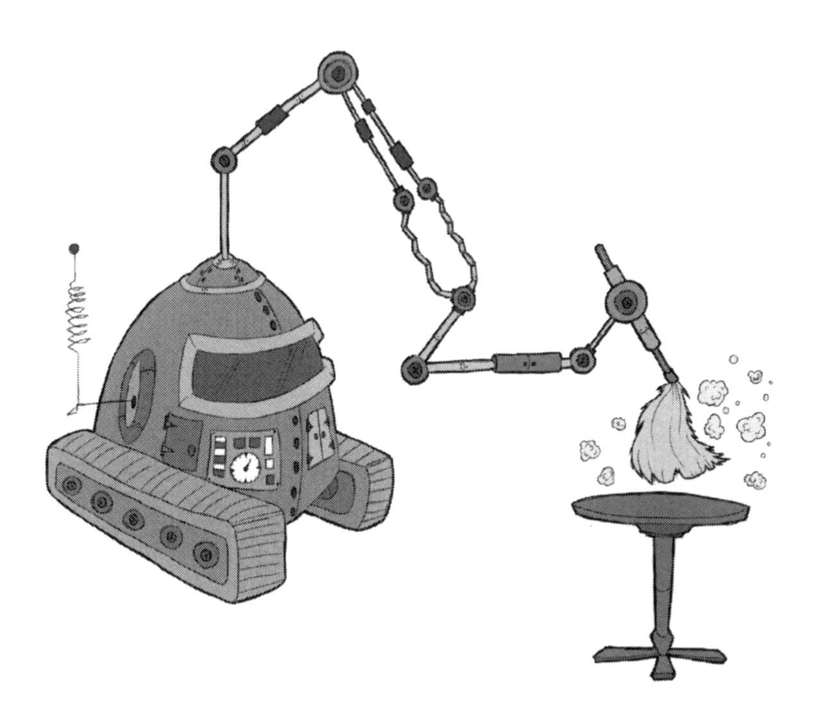

When we flew to California recently, I peeked into the seat pocket in front of me and found treasure: a magazine full of unique items you'd never buy unless bored while strapped to a seat 36,000 feet up. I am not a shopaholic, but these inventions had me wishing I had a third job.

❖ A cushion-keeper to store all my outdoor pillows in one place: only $119.95. Oh, yes. I was telling my husband last week how devilish a chore it is to keep track of those pesky patio cushions that scatter themselves across the wide world. This little storage unit, complete with handles and wheels, is the perfect solution. We'll have to get rid of one of our cars to make room for it in the garage, but at least our cushions will be stored and shielded.

❖ A money sorter that loads up to 130 bills and counts over one thousand per minute: only $199.00. I have been worried about the problem of making money faster than I can count it. This is the solution to my problem of all those fifties and hundreds flying every which way as I try to sort them.

❖ A telescoping chandelier duster: only $149.00 for the basic set, which comes with five cleaning attachments and a handy carrying case. The chandelier in my guest bathroom is the dustiest it's been in weeks, and my downstairs maid will be thrilled with this addition to her cleaning kit. I may even splurge and buy the ostrich duster head for only $24.50 extra.

❖ An eight-color write-on mural of the world: only $149.99. It covers nine feet by thirteen square feet of wall space, but I'm sure Grandma won't mind if we take down her oil paintings, and Mr. Kinkade's print can be hung in the back bedroom. I have always wanted a map of the world I can write on, and this one comes with a dry-erase marker for hours of educational fun. You may hang the panels as one piece or individually in case you just want to write on Antarctica, not on the whole globe.

❖ A marshmallow shooter: only $24.99. Shoots mini marshmallows over thirty feet. Unlike inferior marshmallow shooters, this baby comes with an LED light that aids in locating your target. Complete with easy-to-refill magazine that holds twenty marshmallows (not included). The barrel and magazine are top-rack dishwasher safe. What a relief!

❖ A barbeque branding iron: only $79.95. Now you can find out who's been sneaking in your backyard and cooking on your grill. This stainless steel branding iron will personalize your steaks, burgers, and chicken thighs, so everyone will know who to praise for a meal well done. If you want the custom cedar gift box, it's only an extra $10.00.

Perhaps next time we'll splurge and go first-class. I'd love to see the handy trinkets in those seat pockets.

♥ *From My Heart to Yours: Do you ever dream about having the kind of money to buy silly items like these? I believe it's okay with God if we're rich, as long we aren't covetous. And there's no worry that I'll be coveting your chandelier duster or cushion keeper. I'll be too busy playing with my marshmallow shooter.*

Chapter 38
Name That Kid

I feel sorry for modern kids. Or should I say *kydz*? Today's parents either don't know how to spell or they're trying to be cute.

Not long ago David was always D-A-V-I-D. Little Davey didn't need to spell his name to the librarian, his Sunday school teacher, or the softball coach. Now he totes flashcards and wears a nametag day and night. It might be Dayvid, Davidde, or Daivihd. Same with a perfectly decent name like Mary. Her flashcards could read anything from Mahree to Mayrie to Mairey.

I cringe to think where this generation of creative spellers is leading us. Imagine a family singing together on a road trip. Sister starts, "There was a farmer had a dog and Bingo was his name-o, B-I-N-G-O..."

Brother interrupts, "That's not right. Kevin has a dog named Bingo and they spell it B-E-E-N-G-O-U-G-H." Family bonding takes a huge step backwards.

Or what about Sunday school songs? The leader steps to the podium and charges into, "The B-I-B-L-E, yes that's the book for me..." when a redheaded girl in the front row corrects him.

"We don't spell it that way anymore," she says. "We use the new spelling: B-Y-E-B-I-L-L." The man stumbles off the stage, his hopes for a shining career as a song leader dashed.

I know, I know. Embrace progress, move forward, don't dwell on the past, change is good, etc. I agree. But please don't tell me I'm going to turn on a the Disney channel one day and hear "M-I-K-K-E-E M-O-W-H-S!"

♥ *From My Heart to Yours: Even if you're not thrilled with the name your parents gave you, Jesus has promised to give you a new name when you meet Him face to face. I have a feeling no two will be alike, for we're each unique creations of His, and He loves us as individuals.*

Chapter 39
Housework Is a Man's Job

Inviting people over to eat is one way I force myself to clean house. I don't really hate housework; I just save it for last. After I've finished reading, eating chocolate, writing, going shopping, and eating chocolate—oh, I already said that.

I even read once—in a book by a male cleaning expert, thank you—that housework is a man's job. They are the ones God gifted with upper body muscles, so they can best handle vacuuming, mopping, and scrubbing. Makes sense to me.

Last weekend while zooming along the ceiling with my multicolored cobweb killer, my heart swelled with pride. I was cleaning a whole week before my scheduled dinner party. How efficient I was, how organized, how—*Oh, boogers!* I had dusted a tickle too close to my husband's favorite Thomas Kincade collector's plate and was suddenly staring down at a pile of broken pieces. Once a lovely painting of Christmas carolers on a sunset-washed hill now lay as nothing but shards of useless ceramic. I was so furious I threw away the plate "holder" that hadn't.

Kevin understood, as usual. "It's okay, Honey. We enjoyed it for several years. It was just an accident." However my attitude toward myself wasn't nearly as gracious.

Why had I been so careless? Why hadn't I eaten some chocolate or written an article instead of dusting? Or put that housework book into practice and asked my husband to clean?

I've wondered many times if God has looked down upon the dozens of shards that constitute my broken life. I caused a pile of pain by things I did to myself and others, things I knew were stupid and foolish. Now the picture He'd intended was ruined forever, worthless, good for only the trash can.

Or was it?

Enter God's grace. That lovely quality of His Father's heart that looks at a broken-beyond-repair life and says, "I still value you. I can do something with these pieces. Let's not give up yet."

This is my favorite trait of God: His willingness to redeem. Whatever mess we've made of ourselves, He longs to kneel down amidst the rubble and lovingly piece us together. Even when there are too many jagged bits to fit into the original "painting," God will start fresh, exchanging our brokenness for new life.

If you feel you've ruined your chance ever to be whole and lovely again, please don't despair. God will take your broken shards as a trade-in on a sweet new life. Just sweep them up and hand the pieces to Him. He knows how to fix you.

♥ *From My Heart to Yours: It takes more faith to say, "Fix me, Jesus" than to try to fix ourselves with our own puny resources. Makes about as much sense as women doing all the housework!*

Chapter 40
Top Ten Comic Strips

According to Yahoo! Network contributor Timothy Sexton, newspapers no longer respect the work of serious comic-strip artists. "In the golden age of comic strips, these glorious little snatches of Americana received the full treatment of respect awarded to advertising for toilet paper today," he says. "Comic strips were actually large enough to read and allow the artists to create wondrous worlds. Today's little one inch square panels are an embarrassment. No wonder that any artist worth his salt has eschewed the limitations of newspaper management for the wide-open vistas of the internet."

Mr. Sexton based his list of the top ten mainstream comic strips of all time on their prominence in daily newspapers across the country. Although I don't agree that a couple of his choices are widespread enough to fit everyone's worldview, his was the most conservative list I found.

10. ***B.C .***, Johnny Hart

9. ***The Far Side***, Gary Larson

8. ***Pogo***, Walt Kelly

7. ***Krazy Kat***, George Herriman

6. ***Dick Tracy***, Chester Gould

5. ***Blondie***, Chic Young

4. ***Peanuts,*** Charles Schulz

3. ***Doonesbury***, Gary Trudeau

2. ***Bloom County***, Berkeley Breathed

1. ***Calvin and Hobbes***, Bill Watterson

♥ *From My Heart to Yours: Do you have a favorite comic strip? Make the artist's day by finding their contact information online and writing him or her an email to say,* "You make me laugh. Thank you!"

Chapter 41
A New Holiday Gift Idea

On one of our frequent walks where we talk about everything and nothing, my husband and I discovered a new way to save money and still give thoughtful gifts.

"Isn't today the day you met Jesus, about thirty-nine years ago?" I asked.

Knowing how prone I am to shenanigans, Kevin answered with caution. "Yessss.... Why do you ask?"

"Well, I meant to buy you a gift, but since it's a week till payday, I ate a cookie in your honor instead."

He rolled his eyes. "Thanks a lot. That means the world to me."

"I thought it would. Hey, we could do this for all of our gift-giving from now on. We send a card or an e-mail saying, 'Happy Birthday. We ate a porterhouse steak in your honor,' or 'Congratulations on your new baby; we bought some roses to celebrate.'"

I picked up my stride as I warmed to this brilliant idea. "When our nephew Tim graduates, we can go on that cruise I've always longed for; we can bake a cake and eat it when my friend Terri gets a job; and we can buy a *Get Well Soon* balloon whenever someone we know is in the hospital. Balloons cheer me up; don't they you, Kev?"

Even if he'd folded his answer in half, he couldn't have fit it in, I was yakking so fast. "We'll start a whole new tradition of honoring people on their special day and save money at the same time!"

He shook his head and grinned. "I'm sure it'll go over real big, Honey. I'm just glad the Lord didn't use that method when we needed the gift of salvation. He sent us the real thing, wrapped in baby skin. Now that was a true in-honor gift."

♥ *From My Heart to Yours: One of my top love languages is giving and receiving gifts. But the best gift I can imagine is for someone to give his or her life to save mine. And that's exactly what Jesus did. Not only for me, but for you too. Will you receive His precious gift of life today?*

Chapter 42
Oh, Be Careful Little Nose

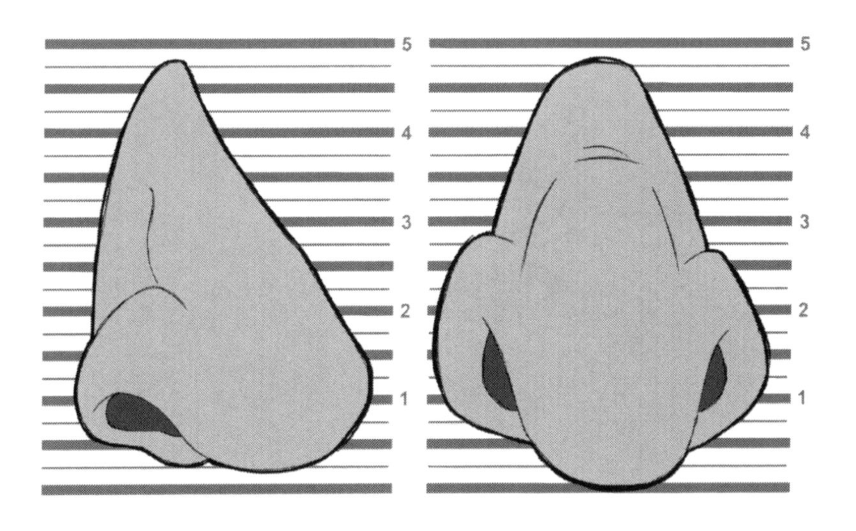

When I bought some anti-viral tissues recently, I noticed instructions on the box bottom. I'm not exaggerating. The makers of these paper hankies want to ensure that they are not responsible for customers ruining their lives or their noses with their product. See for yourself:

"**Directions for Use**: *It is a violation of Federal law to use this product in a manner inconsistent with its labeling. Use only as a facial tissue.*" Oh, I'm so glad you told me this! I was planning on making a boat for my family of seven people and four cats and sailing to Catalina. If I'd done that and it sank, I may have called my lawyer from the bottom of the ocean floor and had him sue you on my behalf.

"**Storage and Disposal**: *Store in a dry area.*" Really? I can't store them in the shower? Rats! "*Dispose of used tissues promptly.*" But I wanted to recycle them. We should all do our part to save trees, don't you think? "*Do not reuse empty container.*" Now this disappoints me. I planned to buy fifty of these boxes, blow my nose till it was raw, and then turn the empty containers into vacation Bible school crafts, like jewelry boxes for the kids to give to Mom or covers for bricks to make decorative doorstops. The possibilities thrilled me. Now you tell me I can't use the empty box. Killjoy!

I wonder what other products come with helpful instructions. Next time I'm at the market, I'll look at the container of twist ties in the produce section….

♥ *From My Heart to Yours: Everyone's logic is different, and I'm sure the makers of these tissues had good reasons for printing these warnings on the box. Since we live in a litigious society, I imagine company lawyers issued memos, along with the EPA's, to the box-design division. But if I knew the logic behind it, I wouldn't have near as much fun mocking them. Sometimes it's best not to ask, "Why?"*

Chapter 43
Faith for Ice Cream

"There they are," I shouted, "in that Dollar General parking lot on the right. Pull in, honey."

We'd taken our daughter's family on a picnic at a historical sight fifty miles from her town. I rode with my daughter and oldest granddaughter in one car, while Kev took the younger two kids in his car. The cars had become separated on the trip home, and since Kevin didn't have a cell phone, we had no way to communicate

I hated to break my word to the kids that I'd take them for ice cream after lunch, so we prayed that somehow God would help us find Kevin and the others. He didn't disappoint us.

"Thanks for waiting," I hollered from my open window. "Shall we go for ice cream after all? We lost only ten minutes or so."

"Sure," Kev said, "we'll meet you at Braum's."

When we settled around our favorite booth in the corner, two-year-old Alyssa grinned wider than a banana split. "I'm happy for ice cream," she chirped.

Then the story of faith for ice cream unfolded. "Daniel was pretty worried that we wouldn't find you and we'd have to go home with no ice cream," Kev told us. "But not Alyssa! She kept saying over and over, 'We *will* go for ice cream; we *will* find Grandma and Mommy and Jenessa; we *are* going for ice cream.'"

I raised my eyebrows and patted Alyssa's back. "Wow, Alyssa, you spoke your faith like Jesus did when He stilled the storm and raised Lazarus from the dead. I'm impressed."

Kevin beamed. "Yep. She believed you'd keep your word to her and was encouraging herself, even when the circumstances looked like it was impossible,"

"I need to take faith lessons from Alyssa," I said. "When things don't look like they're going to happen the way God said, I worry and fret. Only I call it 'being concerned.' But it's the same thing; I doubt if God will come through for me like He told me He would. I need to be more diligent about saying, 'God *will* take care of me. The Lord *will* help me, heal me, provide for me, just like He said. He *will* walk with me and give me victory.'"

Alyssa took her last lick as I finished preaching to myself and said, "And the Lord *will* tell Gramma to take us for ice cream every time you visit!"

Oh, to have the faith of a child!

♥ *From My Heart to Yours: This story of simple, childlike faith encourages me when I'm up against a seemingly impossible situation. I take my Father's Word and cling to it, like Alyssa took my word. And how much more reliable God is than me!*

Chapter 44
The Laughter Diet

You've tried sauna bakes and low-carb, high-protein diet shakes. But have you discovered the slimming properties of a good laugh?

According to the weight-loss experts at 3fatchicks.com, when you laugh your body gets a mini-workout. Researchers claim that for each minute of rigorous laughter, your heart rate increases to the same level as when you walk briskly for ten minutes. But can you make yourself laugh, like you can force yourself to tie on your tennies and head out the door for a jog?

If you can't think of anything funny, try recalling a ridiculous moment from the past that makes you giggle every time you think of it. Listen to a comedy performance on your MP3 player, watch a favorite funny movie, or call a friend who's also trying to lose weight, and tell each other jokes. Even faking laughter can get you started into genuine giggles.

While laughing on purpose has many benefits, it burns only forty to fifty calories per ten to fifteen minutes of laughter. Since fifty calories is about 2.5 percent of the average adult's daily caloric intake, you might want to combine laughter therapy with some more strenuous exercise (no, jogging to the fridge for ice cream doesn't count). It takes me ten minutes on my exercise bike to burn fifty calories, and I'd much rather laugh. I wonder if I laughed while I was riding, would I burn a hundred calories? Hmm…

In addition to the burning of forty to fifty calories per laughing session, laughter releases feel-good hormones that can motivate you to exercise and achieve a more positive outlook. This will improve your mindset if you struggle with self-esteem issues related to real or imagined obesity.

Are you ready to lose some unwanted weight? Let's get started laughing!

♥ *From My Heart to Yours: I wonder if a new industry will result from entrepreneurs discovering the weight-reduction qualities of laughter. Giggle gyms and Snigger spas will spring up on every other corner.*

Chapter 45
Onion "Oops"

When I planted my first garden, I was as green as an onion top. The closest I'd come to gardening was when Grandma Viola sent me out to her berry patch behind the garage to pick strawberries. I was all of six then, so by the time I was ready to garden on my own, a few decades had warped my memory enough to convince me that gardening was simple and sweat-less

When I got my brilliant idea to become a gardener, the Los Angeles suburb we lived in rented spare land from a factory, which in turn rented ten-foot-by-ten-foot plots to gardeners. Although the gardens were over two miles from our house, I figured the rewards would outweigh the travel time. My imagination salivated with images of steaming vegetable stew and bright green salads harvested from our own patch of earth. Naiveté at its worst.

While buying onion sets I wondered why they came in such huge packages. Who needed a hundred onions? *They must know what they're doing,* I thought as I drove to the garden. *Maybe not all of them will come up.*

I pulled out the instructions. "Plant ten inches deep, two inches apart." *How will I ever get them that far into the soil?* I was already muttering, wiping sweat from my forehead, eyes, and neck—and I hadn't even opened the package yet.

I trudged to the car, hunted down a pencil, then stomped back to the garden. All afternoon I punched and jabbed until the final bulb—and I—lay exhausted in the soil.

On the way home a doubt crept in. Had I read the instructions right? At a red light I grabbed the empty package and saw, "ten inches apart, two inches deep." Oh, great. Now what?

Rushing inside the house I called our neighbors, grand-scale gardeners from Kentucky who could make sweet corn grow from a pile of sand and a smile.

"Lucille, what should I do?" I cried. "I planted my onions ten inches deep."

Did I hear a grin hidden behind her sweet Southern drawl? "My lands, child, they'll never come up. You'll have to replant. They'll just sit in the ground and rot."

The following day I tromped back to the garden with another hundred onions. Planting the second set over the first ones, I made sure they were only two inches deep.

I surprised my family a few weeks later with a plateful of lovely green onions on the supper table. I passed them around, grinning. I hardly noticed that I was the only one who ate any.

"Did you forget we don't like onions, Mom?" teased my son. "They look pretty, though. How did you make that fun shade of green for the tops?" I wanted to smack him with my holey gloves.

Instead I swallowed my pride and took a few onions to Lucille, who allowed herself a loud laugh over my crazy planting mistake.

But I had the last laugh when several weeks later the original one hundred onions popped up, their whites a full ten inches long. They were the best onions I'd ever killed myself over.

Since then we've moved to rural Illinois, where I've learned gardening secrets from pros. Funny thing is I've never convinced a one of them to try my ten-inch-deep onion planting method.

♥ *From My Heart to Yours: If at first you don't succeed, read the directions. This applies to life as well as planting onions. I could have saved myself a million tears if I'd only followed God's plan in the first place, instead of trying to do life by my pea-brain methods. Thank the Lord His mercies are new every morning, and He gives me grace in place of my messes.*

Chapter 46
Playdates

"Where's Jenessa?" I asked my daughter during our usual Sunday phone chat. No conversation from Illinois to Oklahoma was complete without a few words from our exuberant granddaughter.

"Oh, she's on a playdate with Abby."

"A playdate?"

"Yes, haven't you heard of that?"

"Well, I've heard of children playing with each other. What makes a playdate different?"

"It's a scheduled time of play. Abby's mom calls and says, 'Can Jenessa come to play next Sunday at two?' It's better than Jenessa seeing Abby making mud pies in her yard and asking if I can take her over there to play."

"You mean you wouldn't let Jenessa make mud pies with Abby on the spur of the moment? You have to plan a mud-pie-making date? Doesn't that take all the fun out of playing?"

"Well, everyone is so busy; it's easier to plan things. Then we don't interrupt people's schedules."

"Goodness gracious," I said. "What is society coming to when we have to plan our play?" I changed the subject before my blood pressure went to the moon. My daughter promised to have Jenessa call us when she returned.

After we hung up I found my calendar. "Phonedate with Jenessa," I wrote in the Sunday square. Then I decided to see if this new system could simplify other parts of our lives.

"Are we going to church tonight?" I asked my husband.

He gave me a hard stare. "Of course we are; I'm the preacher."

I added "Churchdate" to Sunday.

"Would you like supper tonight, Honey?"

Another stare, this time a worried one. "Yes. Why do you ask?"

"Just keeping up with the times," I said. "But that's all we can fit in today. If you want to play after church, you'll have to buy me a bigger calendar."

♥ *From My Heart to Yours: I think the reason we get tripped up on the phrase* playdate *is that those two words seem mutually exclusive. Generally play is something you do spontaneously; a date is something you plan. But I understand that in this fast-paced world, we're forced to schedule our play, which I find not fun. Just give me some crayons and paper or a tub of Playdoh and I'll get my joy back. But don't bother to write it on the schedule.*

Chapter 47
Sweet Tomatoes

As a child I detested tomatoes. Growing up in the heart of Los Angeles County, we never kept a garden, so the only tomatoes I ever tasted were the bitter, tough excuses for salad toppings served at restaurants. Since they were the one food I disliked, my mom was too kind to force me to eat them.

But two or three times a year, I ate out with the family of my friend, Nanette. Her parents rigidly adhered to the "clean your plate" philosophy. If you wanted a trip to Foster Freeze after dinner, you dared not whine about tomatoes in your salad. So I slathered those insipid slices of rubber, masquerading as fruit, with enough salad dressing to host a swim party. And I avoided the horrible red monsters until I was twenty-four.

That's when God took pity on my taste buds and sent me the tomato angels.

It happened on one of Grandma and Granddad's visits to our home when our kids were small. Grandma and Granddad had brought along a few tomatoes they'd homegrown. When Grandma sliced a huge Big Boy, filling a plate with the juicy wedges, she offered me some.

"Nope. I never have liked tomatoes," I reminded her. "That's about the only food—"

Granddad interrupted. "But have you tried garden tomatoes? They don't taste a thing like those hothouse ones served in restaurants. Here, have a slice."

I refused at first, recalling the tomato nastiness forced on me as a child by Nanette's parents. But as I looked at those crimson beauties swimming in their own juice, the sides of my tongue began to prickle. I decided to face down my past and take a taste-bud risk.

"Okay, I'll try one," I said, "but just a wee slice."

When that dime-sized piece hit my tongue, a burst of

sweetness exploded. This wasn't a vegetable or fruit; this was candy in a tomato costume. "This is how a tomato tastes?" I cried. "I've been cheated all my life!"

To their credit Grandma and Granddad never said, "I told you so." But I wouldn't have minded if they had. I've been hooked on those juicy red babies ever since.

I even grow my own.

Recently I asked Kevin to run out to our garden and pick some for me to throw in my lunch bag. He came back with not only a handful of Sweet Baby Girls but also with an observation. "Did you know the tomatoes closest to the stalk get ripe sooner, Jeanette?"

I thought about that as I made my sandwich. "No, I hadn't noticed, but it makes sense. They must get first dibs on the nutrients. "

"Just like in John 15," Kev continued, "where Jesus said if we abide in Him and His words abide in us, we'll bear much fruit."

The older I get the more I realize that I must scoot right up next to the Lord, who is the main stalk, in order to be fruitful. As I seek Him in prayer and His Word, I receive the nourishment I need to grow so I can feed others.

It's not about me—how colorful I look, sweetly I sing, or brightly I smile. It's about making a positive difference in the lives around me by keeping my heart full of Jesus.

Tomatoes, anyone?

♥ *From My Heart to Yours: Whichever way we say it, toe-*may*-toe or toe-*mah*-toe, what matters is the fruit in our lives. I pick the homegrown sweetness of abiding in Jesus.*

Chapter 48
Blessed Bloopers

Since my husband is a pastor, I love stories of pulpit bloopers. Just because you've been called to preach the gospel doesn't mean you never get your *mords wixed.*

As a lawyer-preacher led in prayer, he began his plea with, "Your Honor," instead of "Dear God."

During a confirmation service for new converts, the pastor asked the "new convicts" to come to the front of the church.

Parishioners were amused to witness a man who'd fallen asleep during the sermon jolt awake to the preacher booming, "Where the Scriptures speak, we speak; where the Scriptures are silent, we *sleep.*"

While teaching on the manner of dress of Old Testament priests, the pastor described how bells were put on the bottom of the robes. He asked the class, "Why do you think the priests had to tinkle?"

And here are some of my favorite bloopers from church bulletins.

❖ Barbara remains in the hospital and needs blood donors. She is also having trouble sleeping and requests tapes of Pastor Jack's sermons.

❖ A bean supper will be held on Monday night in the fellowship hall. Music will follow.

❖ Smile and say "hell" to someone who is hard to love.

♥ *From My Heart to Yours: I think churches should be the laughingest places on earth. When God's grace flows through us, we can take a lighthearted approach to just about anything. Life is too short to act like we've been baptized in dill- pickle juice.*

Chapter 49
Quit Pinching My Fruit!

"Oh great," I quietly moan as Mr. Demanding enters my shop. "Lord, give me grace to help him without losing my patience." As the boisterous customer, who believes he's the only person on earth, yaps his orders, I smile and pretend to enjoy serving him. I wonder if there's an easier way to grow the fruit of the Spirit. If only these fruit pinchers would leave me alone.

Just when I think my Peace has matured to a rosy shade of ripeness, Mrs. Hateful pummels it by criticizing my husband. Now it lies in the dust of a pity party, bruised and nicked.

Then there's Kindness. I've prayed and meditated on Scripture to grow it into a plump, sweet offering fit for the King. Mr. Blustery embarrasses me in front of three friends at church. I gaze down at a slimy mass of Annoyance. Foiled again.

I thought Self-Control was coming along nicely. I'd indulged in only one dessert a day for the last three weeks, and hadn't gossiped in twenty-three and a half hours—until Ms. Busybody offered me a plate of fudge and the inside scoop on Mrs. Hateful. How dare she pinch twice!

I could have a basketful of Patient pears, Faithful figs, and Goodness grapes by now if not for all these fruit-pinching brothers and sisters who impede my progress. I think I need to find a quiet plot of land away from civilization where I can cultivate my own private orchard, where no fruit pinchers can find me and ruin my lovely crop, where I can bask in the pride of a well-tended harvest.

Did I say *pride*? Oh, dear. Now I'm pinching my own fruit. Maybe I should revise my initial prayer: "Lord, give me grace not to sabotage my growth."

♥ *From My Heart to Yours: I believe the Lord wants us to pray for the fruit of the Spirit to grow in us. Don't believe the lie that if you pray for patience, God will send you problems. You get problems from being on this sin-filled earth; the Devil just wants you to think they come from God. Go ahead and ask for a fruit-stand full of patience, peace, and all the others. Then tell that fruit-pinchin' devil to keep his hands off your crop, in Jesus' name!*

Chapter 50
Shouting Food

Red-potato salad with green onions shouted at me a few days ago, demanding I ask my husband to make a batch. I was quick to obey. Since Kevin has perfected this recipe to an art form, he was eager to assist me in indulging the food voices.

Don't pretend you don't hear them too. When you are reading in bed at night, the chips you hid from your kids holler to you from the sock drawer. You make sure no lights are oozing from under closed bedroom doors before you slip the drawer open and ease the bag out. You even place each chip on your tongue lightly, allowing it to soak in before biting down. You can't risk waking anyone with loud crunching. Those chips are yours, all yours.

And we're all familiar with singing ice cream, chattering cookies, hollering pizza, and humming donuts. They sneak up behind us as we drive to work, write e-mails, and watch TV. No activity is sacred to these tormenting treats.

Right before I went to sleep last night, one accosted me. "I wish we had some dark chocolate truffles," I said to Kev.

"Sorry, Hon. We have Girl Scout cookies in the pantry. Do you want me to get you some?"

I sighed. "No; thanks anyway. I've had enough sweets today. I just wanted to entertain my tongue. I need to say *no* more often to screaming food."

"Good for you, Jeanette. The Apostle Paul would be proud of you for keeping your body under control. G'nite."

"Wait," I said as I flipped my bedside lamp back on. "I didn't say I was cutting out snacks forever, only that I'd had enough sweets for one day. Can you please get me a bowl of that red-potato salad?"

♥ *From My Heart to Yours: Have you ever fasted in order to humble yourself in prayer? I once fasted from complaining, and it was the most challenging day of my life! But God answered my prayers in a wonderful way. He saw my heart and took pity on me. If you can't fast from food, try fasting a nasty habit sometime, and watch how it changes your heart.*

Chapter 51
Ten Little Confessions

When I was fourteen and got into a little trouble while living with Aunt Joyce and Uncle Dwayne, my Aunt Joyce told me, "Confession is good for the soul." That was over forty years ago, and I've been surprising people with my candor ever since. Why should today be any different?

1. Every morning my husband brings me coffee from freshly ground beans. When he is gone overnight, I tote the programmable coffeemaker into the bedroom and set it on my desk across the room so I can wake up to the smell of coffee brewing. I'm not lazy. I just prefer to use my energy for more important activities, like laughing and watching *Monk* reruns.

2. I spoil my four cats beyond reason, speaking to them in baby talk and letting them climb wherever they want. They even jump on the bathroom counter and drink water from a special cup there. I tell each of them they're my favorite kitty. Please don't let the cat out of the bag and snitch on me.

3. We lived in Illinois six years before I shoveled snow the first time, and that was only because my husband had broken his ankle. In previous years I let him do the shoveling so he could show off his upper body muscles.

4. I not only snort when I laugh very loud, but I also snort when I'm disgusted.

5. I love to slide across the kitchen floor in my stocking feet. You too? I knew it!

6. On my end table I keep several stacks of different colored three-by-five cards with encouraging Scriptures written on them. Every day I pick a stack that matches the outfit I'm wearing and say them aloud.

7. Some days I feel crazy and wild and say Scriptures from cards that clash with my outfit!

8. My husband does most of the cooking at our house, which is fine with me because I am not fond of cooking. My favorite cookbook contains recipes of three, four, and five ingredients.

9. My favorite sport is dining out. Shopping comes a close second. My favorite items to shop for are gift cards for restaurants.

10. My hair is not this bright red naturally. Its original color is auburn, which went bye-bye when I was thirty-five. My youngest granddaughter's hair is the same shade that mine was when I was a child. YES!

♥ *From My Heart to Yours: Ahhh, confession! I do feel better now. Aunt Joyce, you were right.*

Chapter 52
Comical Classifieds

Ever try reading classified ads for a way to add humor to your day? You may discover some laughable ones like these.

- **Doberman pinscher**: smart, young, strong, good guard dog, eats anything, loves children.
- **For sale**: antique desk suitable for lady with thick legs and big drawers.
- **Seeking employment**: Tired of cleaning yourself? Let me do it instead.
- **Used cars**: Why go elsewhere and be cheated? Come here first.
- **Childcare**: Our experienced mom will care for your child. Fenced yard, meals, and smacks included.
- **For sale**: One pair hardly used dentures, only two teeth missing.
- **Soccer ball**: Signed by either Pele′, former Brazilian soccer player widely renowned by most experts and fans to be the finest player that's ever existed, or by some guy named Peter.
- **Tombstone**: Standard gray, a good buy for someone named Grady.
- **Seeking employment**: Man, honest. Will take anything.
- **Wanted:** Someone to go back in time with me. This is not a joke. You'll get paid when we get back. Must bring your own weapons. Safety not guaranteed. I have only done this once before.
- **Turkey for sale:** Partially eaten, only eight days old. Both drumsticks still intact.

And my personal favorite classified:

❖ **Illiterate?** Write today for free help.

♥ *From My Heart to Yours: Most writers of classifieds are common folk wanting to sell an item; they're not English majors. And since most ad managers at newspaper offices don't have time to correct spelling and grammar, the reading makes for some hilarious times.*

Chapter 53
Sign Me Up

I collect silly signs. Not in my garage or basement, but written on a list I can pull out during an Eeyore attitude when I need to laugh. Here are some of my favorites:

- *"Louie's Donut": I always felt sorry for Louie. Once he sold his donut, did he go out of business?*

- *"Do not stand, sit, climb, or lean on zoo fences. If you fall the animals could eat you, and this might make them sick.*" And then the zoo might sue you for animal abuse.

- *"Winter Brings Cold Weather.*" Do you suppose the guys in maintenance were bored the day they put this up on our park-entrance marquee?

- *"Attention, Dog Guardians: pick up after your dogs. Thank you. Attention, Dogs: Grrr, bark, woof! Thank you.*" How kind of them to include the canine half in dog-ese.

- *"Parking Deck*": Not funny? It was when I mistook it at the entrance of a mall for "*Peking Duck."* I told my husband we should try it for dinner. He declined, thinking the ambience beneath us.

- *"Please don't throw your cigarette ends on the floor. The cockroaches are getting cancer.*" I hope this one wasn't posted in a restaurant.

Just as signs direct us, God's Word also guides and protects us, reflecting the Lord's heart. As His children believers are signs to the world. I wonder: What kind of sign am I? A humorous sign, easing someone's burden for a moment? A direction sign, guiding the lost to God's eternal wisdom? Or a reflector, shining with grace from my Father's heart?

My goal? To make a positive difference in the world today, pointing broken people to Jesus. Sure beats that Eeyore attitude.

♥ *From My Heart to Yours: I once mistook a sign that said, "Welcome, Shriners" for "Welcome, Sinners." I thought the church that posted it on their marquee was being very Christlike in its attitude. Perhaps our churches would grow faster if we gave a warm welcome to sinners. We have the answer they need, after all.*

Chapter 54
Swimsuit-Shopping Stress

Trying on a swimsuit was not a biggie when I wore a size six dress and my metabolism was faster than its current *tortoise* setting. Back then I simply picked a color that complimented my skin tone, didn't show too much of what I only wanted my husband to look at, and was half-price.

Now that I am…well, not a size six any longer and may not be again until Jesus returns and gives me my new body, shopping for a swimsuit has reached the number-three spot on my list of high-stress items. (Number one is running out of ice cream, and number two is that we're down to only vanilla.)

I'm not afraid of cellulite, fat, or age spots. I just don't like to advertise them to the world at large—and prove that I am becoming one of the larger ones in that world.

So I torture myself in the dressing room with all manner of spandex-inspired creations that attempt to hide from the younger women what they have to look forward to when they hit the searching-for-my-lost-hormone years and want to eat everything with sugar or fat in the number-one spot on the ingredient list.

I finally decide on a little—and I use this word loosely—number that is busy with sunflowers and hummingbirds I hope will distract eyes from the flesh bulging out of it. I rush to the checkout counter and pay cash so the checker doesn't have time to see what size it is.

In the car I grab my wee scissors from the emergency sewing kit, snip out the label, and then swallow it with a large gulp of diet ice tea. No sense in having it flutter out of the trash bag and let the world in on my dark secret. I can handle the indigestion that results from label-eating; I can't face knowing there's evidence of my swimsuit size somewhere on the planet.

Now I'm prepared for the next time a friend calls, inviting us over to swim. "Let's go," I holler to my honey. "We'll be late for the party!" He comes down the hall wearing the same suit he's owned for twenty-five years, which took him thirty seconds to pick out, try on, and purchase. Makes me sicker than when I swallowed the label.

His eyebrows rise as he points to the old shorts and tee-shirt I have on. "Aren't you going to wear your new bathing suit? You spent all day picking it out and half a paycheck buying it!"

As I tug the tee-shirt down over my hips, I huff like I always do when he's clueless about female logic. "I have it on, Silly, underneath these old gardening clothes. You don't think I'd wear a new tee-shirt and shorts into a chlorinated pool, do you? Now, let's go."

♥ *From My Heart to Yours: The older I get, the more obsessed I become with my body size. Perhaps this is because it's grown and shifted. I'm comforted to know that God looks on my heart, and the larger my heart is, the prouder I make Him.*

Chapter 55
How Old Is Old?

"Original chicken sandwich, buy one get one free," read Kevin as we passed a fast-food restaurant. "Wow, if that sandwich is made from the original chicken, it must be really old!"

Five-year-old Daniel quipped from the back seat, "It might even be older than Grandpa!"

When my grandparents were in their fifties, I remember thinking how old they seemed. Now it seems mighty young. And when as an adult I revisited the enormous church I'd grown up in, I was shocked at how it had shrunk. I was also astounded to discover how much my parents grew in wisdom from the time I was sixteen to my twenty-fifth birthday.

It's all a matter of perspective.

As we grow we realize our childish viewpoints are just that: childish. And if we're wise we'll let go of some of those infantile ideas. For example:

- Circumstances should always go according to my plan.
- I shouldn't have to wait for what I want.
- People are here to make me happy.
- I can get my way by bullying or throwing a hissy fit.
- If you don't agree with me, I won't be your friend.

And we exchange them for ideas like this:

- If I have to switch to Plan B, I'll adjust.
- Waiting for something I really want makes me appreciate it more.

- I am here to help people and bring out the best in them.

- I refuse to manipulate others to get my way; I trust the Lord to give me His best.

- If we always agree with each other, our thinking will never expand.

We all know people whose bodies have aged but whose thinking has remained childish. No one enjoys their company because they're so full of themselves their hearts have no room for anyone else. I don't want to become one of these oldies but moldies, acting like a baby in a grown-up suit. Like the Apostle Paul talks about in 1 Corinthians 12, I want to leave behind childish ways and think like an adult.

Now if I can just convince Daniel to leave behind his idea that Grandpa is old—and by association, that Grandma is old too. In another fifty years or so, he'll change his mind.

♥ *From My Heart to Yours: If I think about me, me, and me most of the time, I'm childish. If I enjoy God's companionship and my life more than I did yesterday, I'm childlike. And that's an attitude that makes Jesus happy.*

Chapter 56
Start Your Day on a Funny Note: Hilarious Newspaper Headlines

When I began writing a bi-weekly column for our local newspaper over a decade ago, I brought the editor a hard copy of my article to work from. This method sometimes led to funny mistakes, like the time they mistyped the title of *Your Mighty Peace* and changed it to *Your Mighty Peach*. I had visions of a diligent farmer struggling under the weight of an enormous peach, hollering for his wife to help him carry it into the kitchen so she could make sixteen pies from it. After that muddle I began emailing my columns to the editor!

Here are some of my favorite headline blunders—from other writers—that went unnoticed:

- "New study of obesity looks for larger test group"
- "Police begin campaign to run down jaywalkers"
- "Two sisters reunited after 18 years in checkout counter"
- "Man Struck by Lightning Faces Battery Charge"
- "One-armed man applauds the kindness of strangers"
- "Survey finds dirtier subway after cleaning jobs were cut"
- "Larger kangaroos leap farther, researchers find"
- "Alcohol ads promote drinking"
- "Safety experts say school bus passengers should be belted"
- "Dealers will hear car talk at noon"
- "Official: Only rain will cure drought"
- "Teen-age girls often have babies fathered by men"

♥ *From My Heart to Yours: Have you ever caught yourself saying something that came out all wrong, the words changing your intended meaning? I wonder if God assigns angels to twist our tongues around occasionally, just to give us fuel for laughter. Perhaps He does the same thing to newspaper editors.*

Chapter 57
Take a Brow

We all have bad-hair days, but did you ever hear of a bad-eyebrow day? I am having one. In fact I have them often lately.

I never worried about my eyebrows until I hired an office assistant who looks like a cross between Taylor Swift and Farrah Fawcett. After looking at her perfectly shaped brows for three weeks, I noticed how my eyebrows tweak off to the side at weird angles, resembling scrub pine trees.

So I decided to help them. You know, shape them a little. No one told me I needed special training.

I didn't want to pluck. I tried that when I was thirteen, and it hurt. I've never believed in the "no pain, no gain" philosophy. Unless I'm in labor and know there's going to be a fuzzyheaded bundle to show for it, I have a great aversion to pain. So plucking was out.

Why not get those stray hairs with the scissors? I thought. *Just a few snips here and there should do it.*

Not.

I ended up looking like I'm shocked on my left side and angry on my right. Which is fine if you look at only one side of my face at a time. Otherwise it appears I can't make up my mind.

Since I didn't own an eyebrow pencil—remember, I'd never given my eyebrows much thought—I got out my eyeliner and started to fill in the missing places. Big mistake.

Gorilla brows now.

Oh, well. Maybe I could serve as a poster person for the International Bad Eyebrow Club and help everyone who works with could-be models feel better about themselves.

Or better yet, fix my eyes on Jesus' face instead of the mirror. Jesus never has a bad day, eyebrow or otherwise.

♥ *From My Heart to Yours: While viewing a TV show that discovers new talent, my friend shocked me with a comment. "That singer's eyebrows are awfully bushy, aren't they?" I hadn't even noticed the woman's eyebrows, since her voice stirred my heart to its depths. And I thought God gave us eyebrows to keep the rain out of our eyes. Silly me.*

Chapter 58
Confessions of a Jailbird

Everyone told me I needed to join Facebook to keep up with family members who lived far away and didn't know what a letter was. I could make new friends who had the same interests as I. It would also help me gain exposure as a writer so people would recognize my name and buy my books. Best of all, they said, it was fun. That last word was all I needed. "Sign me up!" I shouted, logging onto the Facebook site.

At first I accepted friendship requests from every Mabel, Butch, and Greta who breezed onto my profile and offered me a cyber-dark chocolate. Facebook must have known the kinds of people I liked to associate with because they posted suggestions of ones I might want to befriend, complete with a mug shot of each. *How sweet of them to help me gain more friends*, I thought. I spent many merry moments on their site.

Until they put me in jail.

Yep. Seems I had requested friendship of too many people who reported they didn't recognize my mug. Facebook sent me a not-so-merry message, forbidding me for seven days from making new friends in the FB playground. I think it was supposed to make me cry and repent of my too-friendly ways.

What Facebook didn't know was that I came out of the womb with business cards in my wee hand, introducing myself to every nurse, doctor, and aide in the hospital. I planned birthday parties for all the newborns in the nursery and volunteered to be the clown. I came back six weeks later to teach my first *How to Make Friends and Influence Parents* class.

So FB jail didn't scare me. I can make friends anywhere.

♥ *From My Heart to Yours: I've often said that I do ditzy things on purpose to make the rest of you feel better when you act stupid. Then I like to tell on myself to make you feel even smarter and more comfortable. When I reported—on Facebook, of course—that I was in their version of jail, friends came out of the walls to say, "That happened to me, too," and I gained many new friends as a result. It's amazing how a little transparency will endear you to people.*

Chapter 59
Call It Like They See It

When I learned ten minutes into our honeymoon that my husband thought differently than I did, I wasn't surprised. What does surprise me after thirty-eight years of marriage (I was five when I said, "I do") is how we define the same situation. In case you're thinking of getting married and would like some warning—oops, I mean preparedness training—here are a few examples.

She walks into his den and her toenails curl as the surround-sound blasts from his twenty-inch speakers. She calls it "noise." He calls it "sensory participation."

She rises at dawn and peels out of the driveway to spend a day of shopping with her bestie. He refers to it as "debt escalation." She refers to it as "retail therapy."

If she leaves the toast in too long, it's "burnt." If he leaves steaks on the grill too long, they're "blackened."

If she asks, "How do I look?" and he says anything other than "gorgeous," he gets charcoaled toast and leftovers for supper. If he asks, "How do I look?" she takes it as an engraved invitation to point out every lint speck and wayward hair, without any argument from him.

When she drags him to a chick flick, she calls it "sensitivity training." When he tells his buddies about it the next day, he says it was "sappy."

I'm thankful God made us different—indeed I am. I just wish that four decades ago someone had written this article for me. It would have saved us a ton of arguments…ah, I mean discussions.

♥ *From My Heart to Yours: I once heard a wise Bible teacher say, "Make the goal of an argument to better understand your spouse, not to force your opinions on them." That golden nugget has helped us get through many discussions without blasting the other with our marshmallow shooters!*

Chapter 60
Happy Resources to Add More Laughter to Your Life
Online:

- http"//www.rxlaughter.org: Founded by Sherry Dunay Hilber, a former ABC and CBS primetime network programming executive who wanted to use her extensive experience overseeing comedy series to help people in need, Rx Laughter is a 501c3 nonprofit public charity. Initially a start-up research project, Rx Laughter has since expanded into a full therapeutic, educational, and research nonprofit organization that helps people of all ages through the power of comedy.

- http://www.basicjoke.com: Enjoy this collection of funny, clean jokes in hundreds of categories along with humorous quotes, riddles, cartoons, answering-machine messages, one-liners, and more.

- http://www.pbbt.com/Directory/Sites/Clean_Humor is a directory of clean humor sites, appropriate for families.

- http://kcbx.net/~tellswor: Good Clean Fun contains humor of all sorts. No obscene language or vulgarity, just smiles—something this old world needs.

- http://hopeandhumor.wordpress.com: My friend James N. Watkins, one of the funniest people I know in spite of his being an editor, has compiled ninety humorous, hopeful articles written by his favorite comedy and inspirational writers. But of course, I'm one of them!

- http://www.justlaughter.com/laughter_articles.htm offers eight articles on topics related to how laughter helps us physically, mentally, and socially.

In Print:

❖ *Becoming a Humor Being: The Power to Choose a Better Way* by Steve Rizzo (Full Circle Publishing, 2000)

❖ *And God Said…Let There Be Laughter* by Mary Hollingsworth (Guideposts Books, 2008)]

❖ *And God Said…Let There Be More Laughter* by Mary Hollingsworth (Guideposts Books, 2009)

❖ *Humor's Hidden Power: Weapon, Shield and Psychological Salve* by Nichole Force (Braeden Press, 2011)

❖ *Writing with Banana Peels: Principles, Practices, and Pratfalls of Writing Humor* by James N. Watkins (XarisCom, 2009)

❖ *Between Heaven and Mirth: Why Joy, Humor, and Laughter are at the Heart of the Spiritual Life* by James Martin (Harper Collins, 2012)

❖ *L.A.U.G.H.: Using Humor and Play to Help Clients Cope with Stress, Anger, Frustration, and more* by Allen Klein (Wellness Productions and Publishing, 2010)

❖ *Humor as Survival Training for a Stressed-Out World: The 7 Humor Habits Program* by Paul McGhee (AuthorHouse, 2010)

♥ *From My Heart to Yours: My prayer for you is that, with God's help, you find many new "laughing places" and grow in health and joy. With grace and chuckles, Jeanette Levellie*

ABOUT THE AUTHOR

Jeanette Levellie, a recovering perfectionist, manages an office supply store during the day and writes at night. She's published hundreds of newspaper columns, articles, poems, and greeting card verses. This is her second book.

Her lifetime goals include a hot air balloon ride, a cruise to somewhere warmer than Illinois in the winter, and introducing one million people to Jesus. She loves encouraging quotes, dark chocolate, children, making curmudgeons laugh, and cats.

She also loves hearing from readers. Reach her at http://www.jeanettelevellie.com, or find her playing on Facebook or Pinterest.

---

[i] Biel, AL & Bridgewater, CA (1990). Attributes of Likeable Television Commercials. Journal of Advertising Research, vol.30(3), p38–44.

Corham, J. & Christophel, D. M. (1990). The relationship of teachers' use of humor in the classroom to immediacy and student learning. Communication Education, 39, 46-62.